SAN FRANCISCO'S
FISHERMAN'S WHARF

The guardians of Fisherman's Wharf stand watch, *c.* 1979. For the fishermen, seagulls are sacred birds. (Alessandro Baccari collection.)

ON THE FRONT COVER: Fishermen prepare their nets at Fisherman's Wharf, *c.* 1905. See page 38. (Fisherman's Wharf Historical Society.)

ON THE BACK COVER: In 1936, the Pan American China Clipper made one of its routine flights from San Francisco to Hong Kong. In the background is the skyline of the City by the Bay. Pier 39, pictured when ships of the General Steamship line berthed there, is below the plane. See page 99. (Clyde Sunderland Foundation.)

SAN FRANCISCO'S
FISHERMAN'S
WHARF

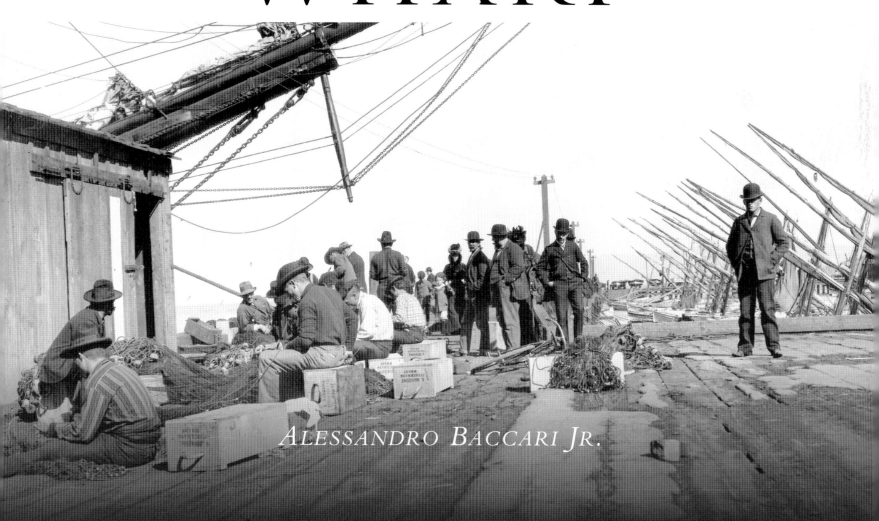

Alessandro Baccari Jr.

Published by Arcadia Publishing
Charleston SC, Chicago IL, Portsmouth NH, San Francisco CA

Printed in the United States of America

Library of Congress Catalog Card Number: 2006923324

For all general information contact Arcadia Publishing at:
Telephone 843-853-2070
Fax 843-853-0044
E-mail sales@arcadiapublishing.com
For customer service and orders:
Toll-Free 1-888-313-2665

Visit us on the Internet at www.arcadiapublishing.com

A fisherman aboard his Monterey boat prepares hooks on line for trawling, c. 1952.

CONTENTS

ACKNOWLEDGMENTS

In compiling this material of the wharf's heritage from the past, I have had valuable help from many sources. Thanks are due, amongst individuals, to: Jim Adams, Frank Alioto, Joseph (Joey) Alioto, Salvatore Alioto, Kirk Bennett, Trevar Booker, Joe Brucia, Ken Burger, Gary Burns, John Caito, Domenic Cannizzaro, Frank Cannizzaro, Paul Capurro, Frances Chu, Angelo Cincotta, Antone G. Cincotta, Stephanie Cincotta, Nancy Conyers, Dianne Cooper, Gordon Cuneo, Tom Creedon, Anthony Cresci, Domenic Cresci, Frank Cresci, Peter Cresci, Rose Anne Cresci, Frank D'Amato, Steve Davenport, Renee Dunn, Thomas C. Escher, Ida Farina, Charles Farruggia, Lillian Ferrua, Patrick Flanagan, Cynthia Foxworth, Peter Francheschi, Sarah Garrone, Mike Geraldi, Salvatore Guardino, Kathrine Higdon, Elizabeth J. Kibbey, William Kooiman, Leo LaRocca, Michael LaRocca, Michael Lannon, Annette Lippi, Robert MacIntosh, Dr. Joseph Maniscalco, Christopher Martin, Charles and Alene Meyers, Kathy Paver, David Pinoni, Jeffrey Pollock, Hedley Prince, Vince Rafello Jr., Kate Richardson, Chester Robbins, Sally Roselli, Ron Ross, Frank Sabella, Lucien Sabella, Mike Sabella, Laureen Sabella, Robert Salvarezza, Peter San Filippo, Al Scoma, Annette (Cincotta) Traverso, and Vince Zanoni. And among organizations, my sincere thanks goes to: California Historical Society, California State Library, Port of San Francisco, San Francisco Maritime National Park Association, San Francisco Maritime National Park Library, San Francisco Public Library, and the Society of California Pioneers.

I am particularly indebted to Pansy Tom for her valued assistance; to John Poultney for the benefit of his editorial knowledge and his confidence in the manuscript; and to my wife, Catherine, for her dedicated guidance and patience in making this book possible.

OPPOSITE: Maintenance workers are seen in this *c.* 1980 photograph inspecting the outer lagoon of Fisherman's Wharf. (Alessandro Baccari collection.)

INTRODUCTION

Since boyhood, I have been attracted to the charms of San Francisco's Fisherman's Wharf. It is one of those rare locations where history, culture, and ethnic pride form a distinctive blend that sets the place apart from others and gives it a strength and vitality all its own. For over 60 years, it has been holding my attention and garnering my affection.

My acquaintance with Fisherman's Wharf began when my grandparents took me there for the opening of crab season in November 1937. I still have fond memories of the occasion. A few years later, I would journey to the wharf regularly with my grammar-school classmates whose fathers were fishermen. Meeting their fathers was always a treat. Miraculously, they always had candy in their pockets for us.

With the outbreak of World War II, silence came to Fisherman's Wharf. In high school during the war years, I began to interview the elderly fishermen. My introduction to them came with my involvement each year in the Blessing of the Fishing Fleet ceremony. I am still involved with the oral history project as well as this ceremony.

After years of affiliation with Fisherman's Wharf, I have become a zealous activist in attempting to preserve its history, culture, and traditions in relationship to the sea.

The purpose of *San Francisco's Fisherman's Wharf* is to tell, in pictures and words, the story of a special place.

The fishing boat *La Ola*, *c.* 1978, secures diesel fuel before going out fishing. (Alessandro Baccari collection.)

The meeting hall of the Crab Boat Owners Association once housed the Genoa Boat Building shop, *c.* 1979. (Alessandro Baccari collection.)

The outer lagoon of the Fisherman's Wharf harbor no longer exists as it did in this *c.* 1980 view. The long building with all the doors, behind the boats, served as lockers to hold the gear of the fishermen. (Alessandro Baccari collection.)

The standard fishing boat at Fisherman's Wharf in the late 1800s was the lateen-rigged felucca, modeled after those used for centuries in Italy. With the advent of the gasoline engine, it was supplanted by the more familiar Monterey fishing boat. (San Francisco Maritime National Park Library.)

Fishing on San Francisco Bay around 1880 are two fishermen and their Italian felucca fishing boat. (California Historical Society.)

The Dungeness crab, arguably the most delectable of all crustaceans, has brought much of San Francisco's Fisherman's Wharf its fame. (Alessandro Baccari collection.)

This is one of the many commercial fishing shacks that graced the inlet shores on San Francisco Bay, c. 1908. (Port of San Francisco.)

This one-man band and singer of sea songs provided entertainment for those who came to buy fish at Fisherman's Wharf in 1925. (San Francisco Maritime National Park Library.)

The taste of cooked Dungeness crab was a memorable experience for a 1977-era visitor to San Francisco's Fisherman's Wharf and still is today. (*San Francisco Chronicle*.)

An aerial photograph of Fisherman's Wharf (*c.* 1956) features Pier 45, the Red and White Fleet, restaurants along Taylor Street, the three lagoons for berthing the fishing boats, Hyde Street Pier before it became a maritime park, Aquatic Park, Muni Pier, and the Golden Gate Bridge. (Aero Photographers.)

Herring fishing on San Francisco Bay, pictured here *c.* 1953, was big business for commercial fishermen from Fisherman's Wharf for many years. (Cresci collection.)

Pictured here in the early 1950s, fishermen often could be seen mending their nets along the docks of Fisherman's Wharf. (Cresci collection.)

OPPOSITE: A felucca fishing boat named *America* is pictured here, *c.* 1891, heading toward the Pacific Ocean from San Francisco Bay. (Fisherman's Wharf Historical Society.)

WHY THE WHARF
IS WHERE IT IS

Before 1840, the shoreline of the northern waterfront ran along the base of Telegraph and Russian Hills, with Black Point cove to the west and North Beach cove to the east. For many years, Meigg's Wharf, built in 1853, was the only major development on the northern waterfront.

This wharf extended out 1,600 feet into the bay from what is now Powell Street. To help control San Francisco's fast-growing waterfront, a State Harbor Commission was established in 1863. Their first task was to supervise construction of a seawall to maintain the edge of the bayshore from

China Basin, on the eastside of the city, to the foot of Taylor Street, transforming the northern waterfront from a series of coves and inlets into a curving shoreline.

Since the water depths of the northern shoreline were generally too shallow for large-scale

shipping vessels, the State Harbor Commission decided to relocate the fishing fleet, which had been berthing at wharves located at the foot of Vallejo, Green, Union, and Filbert Streets, to accommodate the expansion of the shipping industry. In June 1900, the Harbor Commission proclaimed the area between Hyde and Taylor Streets as the new Fisherman's Wharf—homeport for the San Francisco fishing fleet.

If one had the opportunity to look out over the bay from Fisherman's Wharf anytime between the years 1900 and 1914, one would see San Francisco's commercial fishing fleet in its glory years. In those early years, the fleet was composed of lateen-rigged sailboats called feluccas, identified by their triangular sails and manned by immigrants from Italy. Later these vessels were augmented by motors; hence came the Monterey Clipper, a felucca with a one-cylinder, Hicks-gasoline engine and no sail.

In support of the fishermen, the State Harbor Commission, in 1914, had two deep stone seawalls built, not only to hold back the flow of mud but also to serve as wharves for the fishermen to use to mend their nets and sell their fish. The next action the Harbor Commission took for the fishermen was to construct an outer breakwater between Jones and Hyde Streets to form a protected inner lagoon for berthing. In 1919, the Harbor Commission built wharves J-9 and J-10 for the fishing industry. On J-10, a building was constructed to serve as a fish packinghouse, and along the Jones Street Pier off Jefferson Street, sheds were built to house the boatbuilding and boat repair shops of Castaneda, Abruzzi, and Genoa and the machine shop of Bordello and Boss. To aid the fishermen in repairing their boats, the Harbor Commission built a heavy wooden ramp called a "ways," which led up from the inner lagoon to the boat repair building. It was a very entertaining sight watching the fishermen work on their boats.

Today at Fisherman's Wharf, all but a very few Monterey fishing boats are berthed in the harbor. As for feluccas, only a replica of one can be found at the San Francisco National Maritime Museum. As for "ways," it was replaced by a restaurant. Much that was part of the original Fisherman's Wharf came to an end in 1950.

With all the changes taking place, Fisherman's Wharf still remains the best, closest sheltered harbor to bring in a catch from the Pacific Ocean. The wharf also has one of the largest concentrations of fish processors and other services for the commercial fishing industry on the Pacific Coast. About 1,000 people fish for their living out of Fisherman's Wharf.

Here is a panorama of Meigg's Wharf, the city's earliest industrial wharf, built in 1853. It was the first major development built on San Francisco's northern waterfront. It extended 1,600 feet into the bay. Fisherman's Wharf was built years later to the west of Meigg's Wharf. This photograph was taken on January 20, 1884, from Telegraph Hill. (San Francisco Maritime National Park Library.)

A crowd of revelers celebrates Columbus Day at Fisherman's Wharf on November 12, 1938, with the annual grease pole contest. A number of fishermen would enter the contest each year for the prize of $100, which was a good deal of money during the Great Depression. To win, one had to climb a greased pole from the waterline to the top of the pier. (Frank Cresci collection.)

This dramatic *c.* 1872 view shows San Francisco's northern waterfront. The series of coves and inlets would later be transformed into a curving shoreline to be known as Fisherman's Wharf. (California Historical Society.)

The inner lagoon at Fisherman's Wharf is shown here *c.* 1936, with Coit Tower in the background. (San Francisco Maritime National Park Library.)

In 1932, a fleet of Monterey fishing boats are berthed at Fisherman's Wharf. The building in the middle is the Crab Fishermen's Protective Association. (Port of San Francisco.)

An interesting 1865 view of Meigg's Wharf shows the long pier extending 1,600 feet into the bay from Powell Street. (California Historical Society.)

For San Franciscans in the early days of the city, such as these pictured here *c.* 1880, Meigg's Wharf was a very popular place to visit. (San Francisco Maritime National Park Library.)

In this *c.* 1882 photograph, the tall ships berthed in the bay make this a particularly striking view, with Meigg's Wharf prominently in the foreground. (North Beach Museum.)

In the foreground of this *c.* 1864 view, looking towards the Golden Gate Bridge from Telegraph Hill, is the site that would become Aquatic Park and Fisherman's Wharf. (San Francisco Maritime National Park Library.)

The gentleman in the foreground with the silk top hat, pictured here at Meigg's Wharf in 1880, is Abe Warner, proprietor of the famed Cobweb Palace Saloon. It was a place noted for undisturbed cobwebs that festooned the walls of the establishment; hence the name. It was also crammed with oddities and boasted an outdoor mini-zoo. (San Francisco Maritime National Park Library.)

A *c.* 1884 view from the bay shows the newly constructed seawall and Frederick O'Layman's castle on Telegraph Hill, which operated as a restaurant, music hall, and observatory. A cable car brought visitors to the top of the hill. (California Historical Society.)

This view from Nob Hill, *c.* 1867, shows North Beach, Meigg's Wharf, and the San Francisco Bay. (California Historical Society.)

23

Around 1889, lumber is being unloaded off the *Thomas L. Ward*, a schooner, at Meigg's Wharf. (San Francisco Maritime National Park Library.)

Here is the Vallejo Street pier where a number of the felucca fishing boats berthed in the 1880s. This photograph was taken in November 1882. (San Francisco Maritime National Park Library.)

More than 1,000 feluccas plied the San Francisco Bay in 1873. (Fisherman's Wharf Historical Society.)

Returning to the harbor after unloading their catch, fishermen would gather for an hour or two and socialize, as depicted in this *c.* 1900 photograph. (North Beach Museum.)

Fishermen would daily repair their nets along the pier of the small harbor for fishing boats at Meigg's Wharf, pictured here *c.* 1883. (Fisherman's Wharf Historical Society.)

OPPOSITE: This is the Fisherman's Wharf harbor in 1908. (San Francisco Maritime National Park Library.)

TWO

FISHERMAN'S WHARF AND ECHOES OF THE PAST

San Francisco's Fisherman's Wharf is proudly unique among the scenic waterfront attractions of the world. The Fisherman's Wharf of today rests on land created from the rubble of buildings destroyed in the earthquake and fire of 1906. What could not be destroyed was the Italian love of the sea, generations of fishing skill, and traditions expressed in song and good things to eat and drink. It is this heritage of the early Italian fishermen which contributes to today's colorful blending of the old and new at Fisherman's Wharf—the center of an ocean-oriented industry beloved by native San Franciscans and visitors alike.

Those who are privileged to visit San Francisco never fail to recall with pleasure their stroll along this city's historic Fisherman's Wharf. Here they can peer down at the fishing craft gently riding in the calm water or pause to watch fishermen mending a net and listen to Italian-tongued exchanges among the followers of the sea.

There continues the tradition of early San Franciscans who flocked to the beach with baskets on their arm to haggle with the fishermen for the most select of the catch, which they brought ashore. Some of the fishermen families soon began offering cooked crab and other fish delicacies at the boat landing, setting up a stove with a cauldron on top and rough tables at which to sit.

From the days of the gold rush until the end of the 19th century, the San Francisco fishing fleet was composed of lateen-rigged sailboats called feluccas. They were copies of the craft which the Italian fishermen knew in their native land. Green was the prevailing color of the tiny boats, and the name of a patron saint appeared on the hull. The fishermen themselves were as colorful as their craft. Their natural talent for song was to be heard in renditions of arias from Verdi and Puccini, lusty if not always true to the ear. In the fog-shrouded waters outside the Golden Gate, the singing was a means of communication. A companion boat could not be seen because of fog, but one knew it was there.

The original Fisherman's Wharf was located between Clay and Commercial Streets, one block north of the Ferry Building. According to the 1874 city directory, it was from this wharf that the small Italian sails first went out through the Golden Gate to fish for sand dabs, rex sole, round-nosed sole, flounder, halibut, rock cod, salmon, and pompano.

In 1880, Fisherman's Wharf moved down to the India Docks, under the lee side of Telegraph Hill at the foot of Union Street. By 1890, there were over 1,000 feluccas berthed at Fisherman's Wharf. It was referred to as "Italy Harbor." When this dock-land was urgently needed for a large freight pier in 1900, a new Fisherman's Wharf was built at the foot of Taylor Street, outside the area of shipping piers, where movement of small fishing craft would not interfere with other vessel traffic.

The current wharf and the boat basin, with its intricate pattern of J-wharves, were built in 1919.

The feluccas were so arranged that every spar, rope, and sail could be disengaged and, with hatches, bottom boards, and bulkheads, carried ashore. The hull was left an empty shell so that it could be cleaned out.

The crew's accommodations seem to have been the very last thing considered in the design of these boats. The galley consisted only of a small charcoal furnace used for heating, a flatiron, a coffee pot, sauce pans, a frying pan, and some tin cups and plates.

The Italian fisherman wore very heavy shirts and lived in rubber boots that came up to his hips. When drawing the 150-foot-long seine net aboard the craft, the fisherman wore a heavy canvas or rubber apron.

The mainsail of the little fishing boat was its most striking characteristic. It had but one spar, a slender tapering yardarm considerably longer than the boat, made in two pieces and lashed together.

The jib was set as a spinnaker. When before the wind, it could run like the devil; close-hauled it didn't do so well. When it was necessary to remain out overnight, the crew slept in the main hatchway partly under the deck, with some of the hatch covers laid on.

As a rule, the early fishermen fished alone; at times, womenfolk did fish with their men. At the turn of the 19th century, great must have been the excitement in the morning when the boats came in deep in fish, grimy and wet with work, nets in disarray, and the fishermen tired but lustily joyous as if the night of fishing had been successful.

The "second generation" of fishing boats came with the introduction of gasoline engines that were small but dependable "putt-putts." What became known as the Monterey Clipper boats came into general use. The gas engine made it possible to fish more days of the year, gave a wider range for their operation in the ocean water, and provided power to haul in the nets or lines.

Even today, several of the Monterey-type boats remain as part of the fishing fleet. Often likened to the vintage automobiles of the Model T–era, the Monterey Clipper craft sat at harbor alongside a "third generation" of commercial fishing boats—diesel-powered craft, which overshadow them in size, cruising capacity, and are often equipped with two-way radio telephones and sonar depth finders.

In those older days, the fishermen got their news about the weather from nature instead of a radio report. If the moon was in the east, the tide was flowing out the Golden Gate. A circle around the moon meant rain. Porpoises playing around the boat indicated a bad wind was brewing.

Old-timers around Fisherman's Wharf have other tales to tell from the period of the last sailboats used for fishing. It was hard work. If the boat was becalmed, they waited long hours for a breeze or got out the oars and rowed. Sometimes they would throw a grappling hook into the rudder chain of a passing steamer for an easy ride home. When the steamer crews called out imprecations against the marine hitchhikers, the Italian fishermen screamed right back in words that soon became a part of waterfront lingo.

In those earlier periods, the favorite fishing spots were outside the Golden Gate, just beyond the waves breaking the rocks and sandy beaches. It took great skill to manage the boats so they did not drift ashore and wreck. In terms of money, the rewards were very low if today's standards of value are to serve as a measure. The average fisherman earned $2 to $3 a week, sometimes as much as $5. But on the other hand, a loaf of bread could be bought for less than 5¢, and good red wine came from grapes that could be purchased for $5 a ton.

Today, as in the past, it is the fishing fleet that gives Fisherman's Wharf its authenticity and activity—the center of an ocean-oriented industry beloved by native San Franciscans and visitors alike.

Hundreds of feluccas were berthed at the Folsom Street Pier in 1890. These were the first boats to be moved to the Fisherman's Wharf harbor of today when it was established in 1900. (California Historical Society.)

By 1912, the lateen-rigged feluccas were replaced by gasoline-motored Monterey fishing boats at Fisherman's Wharf. (San Francisco Maritime National Park Library.)

Two fishermen are busy painting their fishing boats around 1975, next to Castagnola's Restaurant. (San Francisco Maritime National Park Library.)

Fishermen unload sardines at Fisherman's Wharf around 1936. (Gordon Cuneo collection.)

Sardine unloading could prove a lengthy and tedious process, a fact to which these leftover fish attest. (Gordon Cuneo collection.)

A full boat of sardines returns to port at Fisherman's Wharf, *c.* 1936. (Gordon Cuneo collection.)

Upon returning to harbor, Italian fishermen would often get together and enjoy a meal aboard their feluccas. This gathering took place around 1883. (Fisherman's Wharf Historical Society.)

The Coast Guard building in the background of this *c.* 1938 photograph was eventually replaced by the Fishermen's and Seamen's Memorial Chapel. (Fisherman's Wharf Historical Society.)

This 1912 view of Fisherman's Wharf shows feluccas lined up at the dock. (San Francisco Maritime National Park Library.)

The F. E. Booth Fisheries Packing House was located at Fisherman's Wharf in 1922. From the pier line where lumber was unloaded, the 11.3-acre Pier 45 was built out into the water and completed in 1929. The Booth building today houses the Fisherman's Grotto No. 9 Restaurant. (Frank Alioto collection.)

Monterey fishing boats are berthed at Fisherman's Wharf, *c.* 1935. In the foreground are boat and machine shops and boats waiting to be repaired or repainted. (San Francisco Maritime National Park Library.)

Here is the Fisherman's Wharf harbor, *c.* 1929, while Pier 45 nears completion. (San Francisco Maritime National Park Library.)

Ruth MacLearn Cuneo was born and raised a few blocks from Fisherman's Wharf at 850 North Point Street. The home and family, pictured around 1905, from left to right, are Hazel (sister), George (father), Ruth, Harold (brother), Willamina (mother), and Evelyn (sister). Ruth's husband, Egisto, and his two brothers, Cyrus and Rinaldo, were outstanding artists. Each used Fisherman's Wharf as subject matter and fishermen for character studies. (Gordon Cuneo collection.)

James G. Barron was a chief engineer in the days of the stern-wheelers on San Francisco Bay. He regularly swam at Aquatic Park and was a close friend of a number of the fishermen. When he wasn't on a stern-wheeler, he enjoyed commercial fishing with one of his fishing friends. This photograph was taken around 1890. (Lloyd Barron collection.)

At times, wives would aid their husbands when fishing along the shores of San Francisco Bay. This fisherman's wife was photographed around 1909. (San Francisco Maritime Museum.)

Here is Fisherman's Wharf in 1904, when lumberyards flanked it on the landside. (Fisherman's Wharf Historical Society.)

In 1905, fishermen work on nets at Fisherman's Wharf. (Fisherman's Wharf Historical Society.)

Fisherman's Wharf was once located at the Green Street harbor, *c.* 1896. (San Francisco Maritime National Park Library.)

Feluccas berthed at the old Union Street Wharf, *c.* 1880. In the background is the *W. H. Woodward*, a United States government quarantine boat. (San Francisco Maritime National Park Library.)

The last of the sailing boat fishermen was Artilo Napolitano. His boat, pictured here *c.* 1921, was a "silana," slightly different from a felucca. He died in 1923 when he was about 80 years old. (North Beach Museum.)

The singing of operatic arias made the chore of mending nets easier. (North Beach Museum.)

Here are young apprentice crab fishermen, *c.* 1880. (North Beach Museum.)

Two men fish near the Marin County shores, *c.* 1908. (North Beach Museum.)

A fisherman prepares to go fishing around 1970. (North Beach Museum.)

Up and down Jefferson Street, adjacent to the harbor where the fishing boats were berthed, fishermen could be found dressed in their "Sunday best" mending their nets after attending church with their families, c. 1952. (Alessandro Baccari collection.)

On November 5, 1952, the crab-fishing fleet stood ready for action at Fisherman's Wharf. Rows of crab pots line fishing vessels as they await the opening of crab season. (North Beach Museum.)

The fishing fleet returns to harbor, *c.* 1936. (North Beach Museum.)

Feluccas berthed at Meigg's Wharf, *c.* 1880, in the area known today as Pier 39. (San Francisco Maritime National Park Library.)

Here is Fisherman's Wharf in 1902, with well-dressed fishermen in bowler hats. (North Beach Museum.)

The Chinese fished in San Francisco Bay in Whitehall boats. This photograph was taken around 1908. (San Francisco Maritime National Park Library.)

On April 12, 1906, Chinese laborers load stores and belongings aboard salmon packers to Alaska. (San Francisco Maritime National Park Library.)

The four-masted bark, *Edward Sewell*, sits berthed alongside feluccas at the Vallejo Street Pier, *c.* 1888. (San Francisco Maritime National Park Library.)

Mate Davenport, a bark, was berthed with feluccas at the Vallejo Street Pier, *c.* 1889. (San Francisco Maritime National Park Library.)

On Sundays, the Italian fishermen would play bocce, an ancient bowling game. This photograph was taken around 1936. (North Beach Museum.)

This is Fisherman's Wharf when part of the fleet was located at the Green Street Wharf, *c.* 1884. (San Francisco Maritime National Park Library.)

The Ghirardelli Chocolate Factory stands in the background of Fisherman's Wharf in this *c.* 1908 photograph. (Fisherman's Wharf Historical Society.)

Harbour & Anchorage San Francisco

The Vallejo Street Wharf as viewed around 1884 from Telegraph Hill. Feluccas are berthed in the foreground; the vessel on the left is the SS *Brother Jonathon*. (San Francisco Maritime National Park Library.)

Around 1932, fishing boats would pass Fort Point and the Golden Gate daily, and they still do! Steaming in the background is the SS *Pennsylvania*. (San Francisco Maritime National Park Library.)

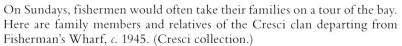

On Sundays, fishermen would often take their families on a tour of the bay. Here are family members and relatives of the Cresci clan departing from Fisherman's Wharf, *c.* 1945. (Cresci collection.)

This is a typical Sunday scene, with fishermen checking their nets, *c.* 1948. (Fisherman's Wharf Historical Society.)

Construction of the fish packinghouse by the State Port Harbor Commission began in October 1918 and was complete by July 1919. The length of the building ran from Hyde Street to Jones Street in an area known today as Fish Alley. In the beginning, it was occupied by four fish companies working side by side—the International Fish Company, Western-California Fish Company, General Fish Company, and Standard Fish Company. With the passing of time, the tenants became Consolidated Fish Company, F. Alioto Fish Company, Puccini Fish Company, and Standard Fish Company. Until the pier—on which the building was constructed—was condemned by the Port of San Francisco, only two wholesale fish companies were in operation there, the Alioto-Lazio Wholesale Fish Company and the California Shellfish Company. This photograph was taken on November 1, 1918. (Port of San Francisco.)

In 1972, the wharf had two petroleum companies, Standard and Mobil, servicing the fishing industry. (Alessandro Baccari collection.)

It took 13 years for the needed breakwater at Fisherman's Wharf to become a reality. That need was first made public in a report submitted by Mayor Joseph Alioto's Citizens Committee for the Preservation and Beautification of Fisherman's Wharf in 1973. Mayor George Moscone, who succeeded Mayor Alioto, tried, with the help of Congressman Phil Burton, to get Congress to appropriate the funds to build it, but all efforts failed. Success came when Mayor Dianne Feinstein secured the assistance of U.S. senator Pete Wilson. Pictured in October 1986 is Mayor Feinstein addressing those assembled for the completion ceremony of the breakwater. (Alessandro Baccari collection.)

Thousands of feet of steel rods and cement went into the building of the Fisherman's Wharf breakwater, pictured here *c.* 1986. (Alessandro Baccari collection.)

Through the efforts of Mayor Dianne Feinstein and U.S. senator Pete Wilson, the much-needed breakwater for Fisherman's Wharf was completed in October 1986. Pictured here is Senator Wilson (third from right), with Mayor Feinstein by his side. (Alessandro Baccari collection.)

In their May 1974 report, the Mayor's Citizens Committee for the Preservation and Beautification of Fisherman's Wharf reported that the most fundamental problem facing Fisherman's Wharf was the surge which was causing frequent damage to boats in the inner harbor and made the outer harbor unusable for permanent berthing. (Alessandro Baccari collection.)

This was the condition of the Hyde Street Pier, *c.* 1974, before the report of the Mayor's Citizens Committee for the Preservation and Beautification of Fisherman's Wharf was made public. (Alessandro Baccari collection.)

It was the neglect of the fishing industry by the Port of San Francisco that led to the formation of the Mayor's Citizens Committee for the Preservation and Beautification of Fisherman's Wharf. This *c.* 1974 photograph illustrates that need; for at the time, the only comfort facilities offered at Fisherman's Wharf for the fishermen were two portable toilets—both of which were in deplorable condition. (Alessandro Baccari collection.)

Another example of neglect was the condition of the fishermen's storage lockers, which became increasingly dilapidated with little or no service maintenance. (Alessandro Baccari collection.)

In May 1974, Mayor Joseph Alioto held a press conference at Fisherman's Wharf to report on the findings of the Mayor's Citizens Committee for the Preservation and Beautification of Fisherman's Wharf, which led to strong editorial support from the media. (Alessandro Baccari collection.)

The construction of the much-needed Fisherman's Wharf breakwater is pictured here c. 1985. (Alessandro Baccari collection.)

The Fisherman's Wharf breakwater was completed in 1986. (Alessandro Baccari collection.)

OPPOSITE: The Hyde Street Auto Ferry Terminal at Fisherman's Wharf opened in 1922 to service Sausalito. In 1927, service to Berkeley was added. This photograph was taken on June 14, 1931, to mark the opening day of the auto ferry service in which motor cars would be transported along with passengers. The service became part of Highway 101. (San Francisco Maritime National Park Library.)

LANDMARKS

Fisherman's Wharf is a San Francisco landmark in and of itself, but within the wharf are also a number of other landmarks. Each has its own story and helps define the history of the area. The main symbolic icon is the wharf's signature sign, standing 32 feet high at the corner of Jefferson and Taylor Streets. The nautical design features a wooden wharf piling with a huge ship's wheel mounted on top and a double-faced, illuminated sign with a rendering of a Dungeness crab and the wording, "Fisherman's Wharf—San Francisco." Without question, this is one of the most photographed signs in the world. It was erected in 1966 by the Fisherman's Wharf Merchants Association and donated to the Port of San Francisco at a ceremony in June of that year.

In addition to this sign, there are 11 landmarks at Fisherman's Wharf whose stories capture the heartbeat of the community and explain why Fisherman's Wharf is the crowning jewel of all of San Francisco's scenic charms. These are the stories of the wharf's landmarks.

AQUATIC PARK: Nestled against Fort Mason on the west and adjacent to Fisherman's Wharf on the east is Aquatic Park, administered by the National Park Service as part of the Golden Gate Recreation Area. It was first known as Black Point Cove, named for the dark laurel on the point. The cove was protected and isolated by steep sand cliffs rising from the water's edge. For a long time, the cove and point were public property, and though it was designated a military reservation in 1850, people began to occupy the vacant land in hopes of establishing title through possession. However, in the late 1850s, the cove became an industrial center, first with the San Francisco Water Company, then the Woolen Mill, which manufactured uniforms, flannels, and blankets for the military. More industry came in 1865, with a smelting operation began there, along with a sulphur-processing plant, an oil refinery, a box factory, and sardine packers.

In addition to the factories, the cove was also used by recreational swimmers. The first formal bathhouse was Joseph Dunkley's Sea Baths, later known as the Neptune Bath-house, perched at the base of a steep sand cliff on the west side of Black Point Cove beach. Other bathhouses followed, such as the Golden Gate Sea Baths and the Sheltered Cove Baths. A daily swimmer at Black Point Cove was William Ralston, president of the Bank of California. On one of his daily trips to the Neptune Bath-house, he faltered while swimming and was pulled from the water dead. Because he was having financial

problems, many felt Ralston committed suicide, but the coroner ruled that he died of a pulmonary embolism. The bathhouse trend continued along the bay shorelines (Bay Street today) between Taylor and Jones Streets, with the North Beach Swimming and Bathing Company and the Triton Swimming Club, a famous resort for the young athletes of San Francisco. By 1900, all of the original businesses had left the area and most of the bathhouses had closed with the arrival of enclosed saltwater bathhouses, such as the Palace Baths, located on Hyde Street, and the Sutro Baths, located at Lands End.

Black Point Cove changed dramatically in the years after 1900, especially after the 1906 quake, when thousands of tons of debris were dumped here and partially filled in the waterway. This trend continued when the Belt Railroad was extended along Jefferson Street to the Pan-Pacific International Exposition in 1915. To reach the expo, the rail ran across a trestle and then through a mile-long tunnel under Fort Mason. The entrance to this tunnel is still visible today. In the 1920s, efforts were underway to convert the area into a recreational water park, a contentious issue that finally coalesced in 1931 during the Depression. A large-scale public works project ensued, culminating in the dedication of Aquatic Park on January 22, 1939. The bathhouse was the crowning achievement, a nautical design with terrazzo floors, a restaurant, a hospital with an operating room, and a 2,000-seat stadium attached. Today the building houses

the Maritime Museum, converted in 1951 as the brainchild of Karl Kortum, and is visited by millions each year. Aquatic Park is listed on the prestigious National Register of Historic Places.

GHIRARDELLI SQUARE, THE CANNERY, AND PIER 39: Millions visit these landmarks each year, each with a personality and history of its own. Ghirardelli Square, named for Domingo Ghirardelli, an Italian immigrant and confectioner, faces the bay with views of the Aquatic Park lagoon and the historic ships at Hyde Street Pier, as well as Angel Island, Belvedere, Sausalito, Alcatraz Island, and Mount Tamalpais. Ghirardelli founded his business in San Francisco in 1852 after an unsuccessful stint as a miner. In 1892, he turned the business over to his sons Domingo, Joseph, and Louis. It was 1894 when they purchased the Woolen Mill property at Black Point Cove for their operation of manufacturing chocolate. In 1915, to coincide with the Panama-Pacific International Exposition of that year, the famed Ghirardelli sign was mounted on the chocolate factory building. It measured 25 feet high and 125 feet long and immediately became a landmark. During World War II, the sign had to be turned off for blackouts, and it remained off until 1964, when it was turned back on for the opening of Ghirardelli Square.

The Cannery shopping center sits partly on the site of Marco Fontana's Del Monte Fruit Cannery and the Haslett Warehouse; these two buildings were separated by an open courtyard where railroad cars were loaded and unloaded. In 1964, these buildings were converted by architects Joseph Esherick and Thomas Church and designer Margaret Larsen into the impressive three-story complex known today, preserving the weathered exterior brick walls and the graceful arched doors and windows.

PIER 39 is a year-round festival marketplace, which hosts millions of visitors annually. The 45-acre complex is built on two levels, with a 300-berth marina and a parking garage located directly across the street to accommodate 1,000 automobiles. A pedestrian bridge connects the garage to PIER 39's second level, or visitors may cross the street on the first level to reach the pier. The location of the pier provides magnificent views of the Golden Gate Bridge, Alcatraz, Angel Island, and San Francisco Bay.

In 1971, it was Warren Simmons who dreamed of transforming a dilapidated pier on the northern waterfront into a uniquely designed "turn-of-the-century fishing village" that would completely encircle the pier from its Embarcadero entrance out to the bay and back. Seven years later, in 1978, his dream was realized, and PIER 39 opened to become the premier tourist destination of San Francisco. Some of the original planking from Pier 37 was used in the construction of PIER 39. Simmons strove to keep as much of the original pier in place as possible in order to meld the old with the new. It cost approximately $54 million to originate and includes a five-acre waterfront park and marina to the west and east of its

entrance. Free year-round entertainment on the pier ranges from jugglers, magicians, and musical groups. And for a day on the bay, it has the Blue and Gold Fleet for sightseeing cruises.

PIERS 45 AND 43: Pier 45 is a major landmark within historic Fisherman's Wharf. This 11.3-acre pier, with its four buildings (each approximately 70,000 square feet), was conceived in 1926 as a mammoth pier to serve the needs of a fast-growing commerce and accommodate the largest freighters. At the center of the pier, a railroad car slip was built for freight transfer, and a lookout station for the Marine Department of the San Francisco Chamber of Commerce was built as well. During World War II, the pier was exclusively used by the United States government; ships sailed with military personnel and supplies for the Pacific theater and returned the wounded and dead. Following the war, the State Harbor Commission, which was administering the Port of San Francisco at the time, applied for a Foreign Trade Zone permit before the Foreign Trade Zones Board in Washington, D.C. Only two previous permits had been granted—one for the city of New York and the other to Mobile, Alabama. On March 10, 1948, Averell Harriman, secretary of commerce and thereby chairman ex-officio of the Federal Foreign Trade Zones Board, presented the charter for Foreign Trade Zone 3 to Thomas Coakley, president of the Board of State Harbor Commissioners for the Port of San Francisco. Harriman stated: "In presenting this

grant to you and to the people of San Francisco, I do so with the assurance that the Department of Commerce will maintain a keen interest in the zone's future welfare and success. We offer our counsel and aid in every possible way to see that this facility is given full opportunity to expand and develop the Port of San Francisco and our world trade."

With the moving of the Foriegn Trade Zone from Pier 45, the port considered utilizing the pier as a passenger terminal with a hotel, shops, and restaurants. Port plans changed with the installation of the breakwater for protection of the fishing fleet. Today Pier 45 serves as the Fisherman's Wharf Seafood Center, housing wholesale fish companies. It is the largest, most modern operation of its kind in the United States. Berthed on the easterly apron of Pier 45 are two historic World War II vessels. One is the SS *Jeremiah O'Brien*, the last active ship in the world that took part in the invasion of northern France and the liberation of Europe on D-Day, June 6, 1944. The other vessel is the USS *Pampanito*, a submarine that was part of the Pacific fleet.

Located adjacent to PIER 39, the Pier 43 ferry arch stands proudly as a reminder of the role it played in the building of a city. It was once the hub for San Francisco's bustling northern waterfront industrial area. Built in 1913, steam locomotives moved back and forth through the arch, pulling freight cars on and off ferryboats arriving from surrounding Bay Area counties. Charles Young, chief engineer for the State

Harbor Commission, designed and built the arch, which houses weights and pulleys that can raise and lower the 100-foot hinged ramp as the water level rises and falls with the tides.

Railcars filled with lumber, livestock, wine, grain, and dairy products unloaded daily at Pier 43 and were ferried back empty for their next load. A network of railroads connected with ferries made it possible to bring these items to San Francisco from every corner of northern California. One of the prime users of Pier 43 was the San Francisco Lumber Company, which leased acres of land adjacent to the pier up until the 1930s. During World War II, it served the armed forces. By mid-1958, the Belt rail service ceased its operation and ferries were no longer used. Since then, the Pier 43 ferry arch has become an architectural landmark.

THE HYDE STREET PIER AND THE HISTORIC VESSELS: The Hyde Street Pier is a place where history takes center stage. Majestic and noble are the vessels of yesterday, each caressed by wind and tide. The vessels berthed here offer visitors much about San Francisco's historic maritime past. Monarch of the pier is the tall sailing ship *Balclutha*, once known as the *Star of Alaska* during her sailing years for the Alaska Packers Association of San Francisco. Built in Scotland in 1886, she was the last sailing vessel in the salmon trade. A few yards away is the lovely *Alma*, a scow schooner built at Hunters Point in San Francisco in 1891 to transport cargoes of hay,

grain, lumber, and building materials. Alongside is the lumber schooner, the *C. A. Thayer,* built in 1895 in Fairhaven, California, for the E. K. Wood Lumber Company. Small, but sturdy, is the remarkable paddle-wheel tug *Eppleton Hall,* built in South Shields, England, in 1914. This steel paddle-wheel tug made history as the last paddle-wheel steamer to cross the Atlantic Ocean. Trim and powerful is the steam tugboat *Hercules.* Built in Camden, New Jersey, in 1907, the vessel towed lock gates to the Panama Canal during her deepwater career. Near the far end of the pier is the steam ferry boat *Eureka,* which began ferrying passengers from the Hyde Street Pier and Sausalito in 1923 and automobiles in 1931, when the service became part of Highway 101. It was the largest passenger and auto ferry on the San Francisco Bay, carrying 2,300 passengers and 120 automobiles.

Linked to the maritime park is the Maritime Museum, located at Beach and Polk Streets. It offers free exhibits of historical photographs and artifacts detailing San Francisco's maritime history from the gold rush era to the present. A few blocks away from the Maritime Museum and across the street from the Hyde Street Pier is the Maritime Visitor Center, located in the historic Haslett Warehouse, now home of the Argonaut Hotel. Exhibits in the 10,000-square-foot visitor center capture San Francisco's maritime past through hands-on artifacts, high-tech interactive displays, and the original 1855 First Order Fresnel lens from the Farallon Island lighthouse. For those

eager to learn more and see more, thousands of books, photographs, and documents make the Maritime Library the first stop for west coast maritime history research. The Maritime Library is located in Building E at Fort Mason Center. Without question, the San Francisco Maritime National Historical Park is the most rewarding of all the landmarks within Fisherman's Wharf to visit.

CABLE CARS AND TROLLEY CARS: San Francisco's historic cable cars and trolley cars are an accepted mode of daily transportation for San Franciscans, an eagerly sought-after adventure for every visitor. Inventor Andrew Hallidie, a Scottish engineer and wire-rope manufacturer, designed the cable railway by which an engaged cable in a slot would carry a car uphill or down at the same speed. On August 2, 1873, at 5:00 a.m., Hallidie triumphantly made the first run from the top of Nob Hill safely down steep Clay Street to the wonderment of the doubting spectators. The two cable car lines serving Fisherman's Wharf are the Powell–Mason line and the Powell–Hyde line. The Powell–Mason line has been serving Fisherman's Wharf since 1888; the other since 1891.

In February 1964, these unique San Francisco cable cars were named a National Historic Landmark by the United States Interior Department's National Park Service. Despite their landmark designation and the city charter amendments protecting them, since 1947, there have been repeated moves to abolish the cable cars and replace them with modern diesel buses. Fortunately for San Francisco, an indignant populace has beaten back each attempt, led by a charming public-spirited physician's wife, Mrs. Hans (Friedel) Klussmann and her Citizens Committee to Save the Cable Cars. Frieda, as she was affectionately known to all, and her group out-maneuvered and out-fought city hall bureaucrats intent on stripping San Francisco of its cable cars during the critical years from 1947 to 1954. Their greatest victory was in 1954 when they obtained enough signatures for an initiative on the ballot, which approved an amendment to the city charter assuring perpetuation of the existing cable car lines.

The F-Line trolley to Fisherman's Wharf is the most successful vintage rail ever opened, with a terminus at Jones Street between Beach and Jefferson Streets. Thousands of San Franciscans and visitors ride the line daily. The idea of riding vintage streetcars from different countries and various cities in America has caught the fancy and the imagination of the riders. The concept for the F-Line, with its historical international and domestic trolley cars, is the by-product of an idea which emerged from the transportation committee of the San Francisco Chamber of Commerce, headed at the time by Rick Laubscher, a journalist-turned-public relations executive. One never knows what kind of car might come along next, whether it would be a streetcar from Portugal, a tram from Australia,

an open-topped "boat tram" from England, or a 1910 Municipal Railway original.

Three individuals deserve the gratitude of the Fisherman's Wharf community for the benefits now being derived from the F-Line trolley service. The first would be Tom Creedon, who, at the time, was president of the Fisherman's Wharf Merchants Association. His leadership was indispensable. The second is the late Don Chee, who, on behalf of the San Francisco Municipal Railway, was in charge of the construction of the extension. With great commitment, he made sure the concerns of the merchants of Fisherman's Wharf were never neglected. The third is Rick Laubscher, president of the Market Street Railway Company, who conceived of the idea for the F-Line and the extension of the line to Fisherman's Wharf.

THE LONGSHOREMEN'S MEMORIAL BUILDING AND BUFANO'S STATUE OF ST. FRANCIS OF ASSISI: One of the architectural splendors at Fisherman's Wharf is the San Francisco Bay Area Longshoremen's Memorial Building. The building was unveiled to the general public on January 17, 1959. It stands as a memorial to the longshoremen on the West Coast who have died, to those who work on the waterfront today, and to those who will follow. Ninety-six reinforced concrete triangles, each 20 feet long, were interlaced and interlocked to form the dome of the auditorium and hiring hall. The dome is sheathed in copper for a combination

of weatherproofing and beauty, rising 48 feet above the terrazzo floor. The building contains a dispatch area, a dispatch mezzanine office, and a concrete balcony for auditorium seating. The auditorium, which can seat 2,300 people, is used on occasion for conferences, concerts, and sporting events.

The late Harry Bridges, who was for so many years the president of the International Longshoremen's and Warehousemen's Union, wrote the following about the building: "Within the shadow of the Golden Gate Bridge and in sight of the ships as they steam inward and outward, the building with its great copper dome is more than a memorial to the men who built the union and the members who carry on its traditions. It is a symbol of the spirit that made San Francisco a union town. It is also a symbol of hope and determination for the future and a declaration of faith in that future." Until his death, Bridges served as a member of the San Francisco Port Commission. As a commissioner, he was a very strong supporter of the preservation and beautification of Fisherman's Wharf.

It was also Bridges who, in 1962, arranged for the internationally acclaimed granite statue of St. Francis of Assisi by the famed sculptor Beniamino Bufano, to be brought to Fisherman's Wharf, where it stands behind a fountain a few yards from the Longshoremen's Memorial Building. The statue stands 18 feet tall and weighs 12.5 tons. It is a majestic work of art, showing the saint with his arms flung out in graceful benediction.

In 1928, while the statue was being exhibited in Paris, where Bufano sculpted it, the late English art critic Roger Fry wrote that it was "the most significant piece of sculpture done within 500 years." The statue was brought to San Francisco in 1955 through the efforts of Bufano's close friend Paul Verdier, owner of the City of Paris department store, mayor Elmer Robinson, and the French government. In 1952, the author Henry Miller wrote this passage in an introduction to an art book on Bufano's sculpture, mosaics, and drawings, "He will outlive our civilization and probably be better known, better understood, both as man and artist, five thousand years hence."

FISHERMEN'S AND SEAMEN'S MEMORIAL CHAPEL: For generations, the fishermen of Fisherman's Wharf have battled the cold Pacific waters, blinding fog, and howling wind to harvest fish from the ocean. In the process, many have lost their lives. In tribute to the men of the sea who have contributed so much to enrich San Francisco's maritime heritage and to honor the memory of those who have lost their lives at sea, the Fishermen's and Seamen's Memorial Chapel was started in 1978 and completed in 1981. Located across from Pier 45 and overlooking the fishing boat basin, stands one of San Francisco's most beautiful and little-known landmarks.

The walls of this vibrant structure bear plaques with the names of hundreds of men and women who have died at sea. Flags and banners hang from the ceiling of the chapel, attesting to the numerous religions that use the chapel. In seaports throughout the world, monuments stand as blessings, as vigils, and as remembrance to those who for generations have dedicated their lives to the sea and its harvests. San Francisco's Fishermen's and Seamen's Memorial Chapel is the fulfillment of a debt of gratitude long overdue to the fishermen who have enriched San Francisco's heritage.

This is the San Francisco Woolen Factory as it was in 1867. Today it is the site of Ghirardelli Square. (San Francisco Maritime National Park Library.)

Here is Aquatic Park cove, *c.* 1886, with its sheltered beach where man and beast enjoyed the saltwater surf with tranquility. The shoreline at this time was where Beach Street is today. Following the aftermath of the 1906 earthquake and fire, the waterway was filled in when the city used the area to dump debris. (San Francisco Maritime National Park Library.)

This *c.* 1925 construction sign promotes the soon-to-be Aquatic Park. (San Francisco Public Library.)

Italian fishermen from Fisherman's Wharf are aboard the *Star of Alaska* on their way to Alaska to catch salmon during the summer months, *c.* 1906. This ship is now the *Balclutha* and is on public display at the Maritime National Park Hyde Street Pier. (San Francisco Maritime National Park Library.)

San Francisco's Aquatic Park has a lot going for it—a pier full of historical ships, a cable car turntable in a Victorian setting, and a procession of ocean-going liners. Ghirardelli Square is a block to the west; The Cannery a block to the east. This photograph shows the National Maritime Park as a state park, *c.* 1975. (San Francisco Convention and Visitors Bureau.)

On September 21, 1909, the *Star of Russia* is on its way to Alaska, bringing fishermen to work for the fish-canning plants. (Fisherman's Wharf Historical Society.)

In 1914, a railroad trestle was built across the waterway of Aquatic Park cove along with a one-mile tunnel through Black Point Hill to the marina district by the Belt Railroad for transporting vast amounts of material needed for the structures and exhibits of the Panama-Pacific International Exposition. (San Francisco Maritime National Park Library.)

Here is a view of the Aquatic Park railroad trestle upon its completion in 1914. During World War I and World War II, it was heavily used to transport personnel and equipment. Plans call for reopening the tunnel to Fort Mason and for the Municipal Railway to run either the F-Line or E-Line, with their historical trolley cars connecting all points along the waterfront with the Marina District. (San Francisco Public Library.)

This is the barge office at Meigg's Wharf around 1880. (San Francisco Public Library.)

This is the South End Rowing Club building before it was moved to the east side of Aquatic Park, *c.* 1908. (San Francisco Maritime National Park Library.)

Each year, the members of the Crab Fisherman's Protection Association would celebrate Columbus Day at Aquatic Park with swimming and rowing events, followed by a boat parade on the bay and picnic in Sausalito. This photograph was taken around 1917. (California State Library.)

In 1908, Pres. Theodore Roosevelt's Great White Fleet anchored in San Francisco Bay for a week's visit. The fleet was on an around-the-world tour. The naval vessels were painted white for this special tour. (Gordon Cuneo collection.)

Here is Pres. Theodore Roosevelt's Great White Fleet exiting the San Francisco Bay in 1908. In the foreground is the California Fruit Packers Association cannery (later to be called the Del Monte cannery). (Gordon Cuneo collection.)

Salmon fishermen from Fisherman's Wharf are onboard the *Star of Alaska* entering Chignik Bay, Alaska, *c.* 1905.(San Francisco Maritime National Park Library.)

Challenging the chilly waters of San Francisco Bay in the annual swim of the Golden Gate are these hardy members of the Dolphin Swim and Boating Club, located at Aquatic Park, *c.* 1941. (Vincent Cresci collection.)

The San Francisco fishing fleet participates in a funeral service at sea, *c*. 1938, for one of their fellow fishermen. (Alessandro Baccari collection.)

Mourners remember a fellow fisherman lost at sea with prayers and floral tributes, *c*. 1938. (Alessandro Baccari collection.)

The Fishermen's and Seamen's Memorial Chapel, the long-awaited shrine to the memory of fishermen who lost their lives at sea, was completed in 1981. The chapel is located adjacent to Pier 45 at Fisherman's Wharf on the site of the old Coast Guard building. Rescue missions for foundering vessels were once sent from here. (Alessandro Baccari collection.)

The Madonna del Lume (Mother of Light) Blessing of the Fishing Fleet Ceremony has taken place on the first Sunday in October since 1935. As part of the observance, a solemn high mass is held at Saints Peter and Paul Church, followed by an eight-block procession that includes a painting of the Madonna mounted on a flower-covered float to Fisherman's Wharf. At the wharf, the pastor of the church sprinkles holy water on the fishing boats and prays for an abundance of fish and protection. This photograph was taken c. 1959. (Frank Cresci collection.)

Hundreds march in the religious procession from Saints Peter and Paul Church in North Beach to Fisherman's Wharf to take part in the Blessing of the Fishing Fleet ceremony. This is a photograph of the 1959 event when Rev. Fr. Gabriel Zavattaro, S.D.B., pastor of the church, led the procession. (Frank Cresci collection.)

Children of fishermen take part in the annual Madonna del Lume (Mother of Light) Blessing of the Fishing Fleet Ceremony, c. 1959. (Frank Cresci collection.)

Marching in procession from Saints Peter and Paul Church to Fisherman's Wharf, *c.* 1955, are members of the Madonna del Lume Society, sponsors of the Blessing of the Fishing Fleet ceremony. (Frank Cresci collection.)

Rev. Fr. Louis Masoero, pastor of Saints Peter and Paul Church, blesses the fishing boats during the 1969 Madonna del Lume (Mother of Light) celebration at Fisherman's Wharf. (Alessandro Baccari collection.)

Pictured at the 1982 Madonna del Lume Celebration, from left to right, are Frances Tarantino, president of the Madonna del Lume Society; Maria Rosa San Filippo, queen of the 1982 celebration, with her father, Salvatore San Filippo, holding the banner of the society; and Rosa Castelloni, cofounder of the Madonna del Lume Society and celebration. (Alessandro Baccari collection.)

Hundreds of fishermen and their families attended the memorial service for Jack Favaloro, Thomas McCarthy, and Vincenzo Ingargiola, who were lost at sea in 1986 when the *Jack Jr.*, a 72-foot trawler, was struck by a freighter in dense fog. (Alessandro Baccari collection.)

The tragedy of the sinking of the trawler *Jack Jr.* in 1986, which took three lives, pained the community of fishermen at Fisherman's Wharf, especially since the freighter that hit the vessel left the scene of the accident without offering aid to the drowning men. Capt. Joseph Cattolica is pictured here being interviewed by Jim Kelly, a reporter for the *San Francisco Progress*. (Alessandro Baccari collection.)

Fisherman Frank D'Amato, his wife, Lillian, and mother-in-law, Phyllis Ramirez, joined other fishermen and their families attending the memorial service for those lost at sea in 1986. (Alessandro Baccari collection.)

A memorial service was held at sea for the fishermen lost in the sinking of the *Jack Jr.* in 1986. Families of those who drowned in the accident are shown here aboard the *Western Seas*, along with members of the press. (Alessandro Baccari collection.)

Sorrow is etched on the faces of Mrs. Jack Favaloro (in black shawl, center) and her family as they mourn the loss of her husband, who drowned with two of his crew members when his boat, the *Jack Jr.*, was struck by a freighter while they were fishing in 1986. (Alessandro Baccari collection.)

Prior to the memorial service at sea for the fishermen who drowned when the *Jack Jr.* fishing trawler was struck, a mass was held at the Fishermen's and Seamen's Memorial Chapel. Pictured attending the service were the following Fisherman's Wharf community leaders, from left to right, (first row) Lu Hurley, president of Hurley Helicopter Service; and Steve and Frances Tarantino, representing the Madonna del Lume Society; (second row) Don Maskell, president of Maskell Marine Services; Christopher Martin, president of The Cannery; Steven Giraudo, president of Boudin Bakeries; and Patrick Flanagan, president of Standard Fisheries and of the Fisherman's Wharf Merchants Association. (Alessandro Baccari collection.)

Patrick Flanagan, president of Standard Fisheries and the Fisherman's Wharf Merchants Association (shown in the center), organized the memorial service for the three fishermen who drowned when their vessel, the *Jack Jr.*, was struck by a freighter a few miles outside the Golden Gate Bridge. Flanagan is pictured here discussing the tragedy with newspaper reporter Jim Kelly and Christopher Martin, president of The Cannery and vice-president of the Fisherman's Wharf Merchants Association. (Alessandro Baccari collection.)

Each vessel that participated in the 1986 memorial service at sea brought floral tributes that were cast into the ocean. (Alessandro Baccari collection.)

A crew member of the vessel *St. Francis* readies himself to cast a floral tribute into the ocean to honor the memory of those who drowned when the *Jack Jr.* sunk. (Alessandro Baccari collection.)

Rev. Fr. Armand Oliveri, S.D.B., pastor of Saints Peter and Paul Church, played a major role in counseling the families of the ones lost with the sinking of the fishing trawler *Jack Jr.* in 1986. (Alessandro Baccari collection.)

The San Francisco fishing fleet attended the 1986 memorial service at sea for those who died aboard the *Jack Jr.* (Alessandro Baccari collection.)

Each year, the Madonna del Lume (Mother of Light) Society stages a two-day celebration at Fisherman's Wharf during the first weekend in October. On Saturday, there is a mass at the Fishermen's and Seamen's Memorial Chapel, followed by a service at sea. On Sunday, there is a mass at Saints Peter and Paul Church, followed by a procession from the church to Fisherman's Wharf for the blessing of the boats. Pictured here *c.* 1996 is the fishing fleet with family members onboard for the service at sea. (Alessandro Baccari collection.)

Every year on the first Saturday in October, crews of the fishing fleet from San Francisco's Fisherman's Wharf honor the memory of their fellow fishermen who died at sea with a memorial service outside the Golden Gate. This photograph of the fleet was taken *c.* 1996. (Alessandro Baccari collection.)

Rev. Fr. Armand Oliveri, S.D.B., of Saints Peter and Paul Church celebrates mass at the Fishermen's and Seamen's Memorial Chapel for the members of the Madonna del Lume Society. The event, pictured here *c.* 1981, marked the first annual memorial service. (Alessandro Baccari collection.)

The San Francisco fishing fleet returns from the 1986 memorial service outside the Golden Gate to honor the memory of fishermen lost at sea. (Alessandro Baccari collection.)

The Fishermen's and Seamen's Memorial Chapel was started in 1978 and completed in 1982. The chapel honors the memory of those who lost their lives at sea. Flags and banners hang from the ceiling of the chapel, attesting to the numerous religions that use the chapel. The first Roman Catholic mass at the chapel was celebrated in 1981 (before completion) by Rev. Fr. Gabriel Zavattaro, S.D.B., pastor of Saints Peter and Paul Church and one of the prime supporters for the chapel. (Alessandro Baccari collection.)

Harry Bridges, president of the International Longshoremen's and Warehousemen's Union in 1962, arranged for the internationally acclaimed granite statue of St. Francis of Assisi by sculptor Beniamino Bufano to be brought to Fisherman's Wharf and erected next to the Longshoremen's Memorial Building. Pictured here is Bufano in his studio with a replica of the statue. (Alessandro Baccari collection.)

Harry Bridges, who served for many years as president of the International Longshoremen's and Warehousemen's Union, was one of the great labor leaders of the 20th century. As a member of the San Francisco Port Commission, he was a very strong supporter for the preservation and beautification of Fisherman's Wharf. Through his efforts, the construction of the Fisherman's and Seamen's Memorial Chapel was made possible, and it was Bridges who selected the Fisherman's Wharf site for the Longshoremen's Memorial Building. Here he is during the famed waterfront strike of 1936. (Alessandro Baccari collection.)

The longshoremen's strike of 1936 paralyzed the San Francisco waterfront as ships could not be loaded or unloaded. Union men were killed during the strike. The Longshoremen's Memorial Building at Fisherman's Wharf is a tribute to the men who built the union and to those who carry on its traditions. Here maritime picketers lined up four deep, waiting their turn to be fed by the union. (Alessandro Baccari collection.)

During the San Francisco waterfront strike of 1936, longshoremen improvised dozens of these shacks for shelter against the elements of the weather when on the picket line. The Longshoremen's Memorial Building at Fisherman's Wharf preserves their story and serves as a tribute to those who built the union and for those who carry on the union's traditions. (Alessandro Baccari collection.)

Railcars filled with lumber, livestock, wine, grain, and dairy products unloaded daily at Pier 43, built in 1913. The San Francisco Lumber Company was one of its main users. This photograph was taken in 1916. (San Francisco Maritime National Park Library.)

Pier 43 played a major role in the building of the *City of San Francisco*, which was identified as the Western Pacific Railroad barge and ferry ship. The arch houses weights and pulleys that can lift and lower the 100-foot ramp as the water level rises and falls with the tides. This photograph was taken around 1923. (Alessandro Baccari collection.)

Today Pier 39 is a year-round festival marketplace within a five-acre waterfront park and marina. Prior to its current use, it was home for many years to the General Steamship Company. This is a look at Pier 39 in 1920. (San Francisco Maritime National Park Library.)

Warehouses, railroad tracks, lumberyards, and piers filled with tall ships and steamships best describe the scene of the northern waterfront in 1919. The warehouse in the foreground stored medical army supplies and the pump house for the Spring Water Company. In the background of this 1919 photograph are Piers 37, 39, and 41. (Port of San Francisco.)

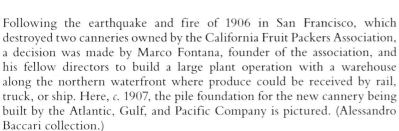

By 1915, the California Fruit Packers Association was the largest packer of canned fruits and vegetables in the world. Marco Fontana, who created the cannery, died in 1922. This is what the plant operation looked like the year of his death. (Alessandro Baccari collection.)

Following the earthquake and fire of 1906 in San Francisco, which destroyed two canneries owned by the California Fruit Packers Association, a decision was made by Marco Fontana, founder of the association, and his fellow directors to build a large plant operation with a warehouse along the northern waterfront where produce could be received by rail, truck, or ship. Here, *c.* 1907, the pile foundation for the new cannery being built by the Atlantic, Gulf, and Pacific Company is pictured. (Alessandro Baccari collection.)

This view shows the California Fruit Packers Association cannery from the bay, *c.* 1910. (The Cannery collection.)

In 1909, workers at the California Fruit Packers Association plant at Fisherman's Wharf received 40¢ an hour. (The Cannery collection.)

Several thousand people worked for the California Fruit Packers Association in 1910. (The Cannery collection.)

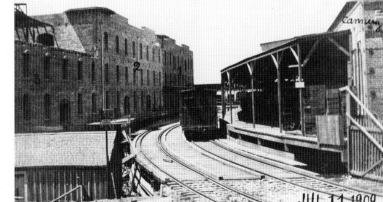

Thirty to 40 railroad cars per day would bring in fruits and vegetables for processing and canning at America's largest cannery, owned and operated by the California Fruit Packers Association, pictured here *c.* 1909. (The Cannery collection.)

In 1916, "Del Monte" became the brand name for the California Fruit Packers Association. To celebrate the announcement of the brand name, the company held a Sunday picnic outing for the employees. (Alessandro Baccari collection.)

Leonard Martin, who established The Cannery Shopping Center, purchased a double-decker London bus to move people back and forth from The Cannery and Ghirardelli Square and to tour Fisherman's Wharf. Pictured here around 1968, it became a popular attraction for The Cannery. (The Cannery collection.)

Workers at Ghirardelli, *c.* 1900, are shown molding and packing cake chocolate in the North Point factory. (The Ghirardelli Square collection.)

This view shows the Ghirardelli Chocolate Factory from the waterway of Aquatic Park, *c.* 1920. The railroad track along Jefferson Street was the plant's main transportation method for receiving goods. The electrical sign on the building was installed in 1915 to coincide with the Panama-Pacific International Exposition of that year. (The Ghirardelli Square collection.)

A San Francisco landmark was the Standard service station, which was located at the corner of Jefferson and Taylor Streets for nearly 60 years. Before construction of the station with its nautical design, the property was used by the San Francisco Lumber Company. The station is seen here on June 6, 1924, in this photograph by John W. Proctor. (San Francisco Maritime National Park Library.)

Here is Fisherman's Wharf in 1938. In the background is Pier 45 with the *Matsonia* passenger vessel being unloaded. It sailed back and forth to Hawaii from San Francisco and Los Angeles. Berthed across the lagoon in front of the *Matsonia* are sardine fishing boats. (Library of Congress Photograph Library.)

A 1984 celebration at Fisherman's Wharf marks the cable cars' return to service after a two-year absence while the system was being rebuilt. In this photograph, Virgil Caselli, who was then general manager of Ghirardelli Square and chairman of the San Francisco Committee to Save the Cable Cars, was at the podium. He had just introduced Mrs. Hans (Friedel) Klussmann, who spearheaded the effort. Without her civic leadership, there might not be cable cars in San Francisco today. (Fisherman's Wharf Historical Society.)

The SS *Jeremiah O'Brien*, docked at Pier 45 in the heart of Fisherman's Wharf, is a working ship and a living museum dedicated to preserving the history of the patriotic, brave men and women who built, sailed, and defended the liberty ships during World War II. Built by the New England Shipbuilding Corporation in South Portland, Maine, the keel was laid on May 6, 1943, and was launched on June 19, 1943. During the war, the ship operated for the government by the Grace Lines. She made 11 trips back and forth from England to the invasion beaches in France. Her 12th trip across the English Channel in 1994 was to mark the 50th anniversary of the Normandy Invasion. Of all the vessels that participated in the ceremony, the SS *Jeremiah O'Brien* was the only vessel that had actually been to Normandy to support the Allied assault. (National Liberty Ship Memorial collection.)

Crew members are aboard the USS *Pampanito* at Midway Island in May 1944. Sailors who pulled into the island between patrols called it "Gooneyville," because one of the only things to do was watch the clumsy takeoffs and landings of resident gooney birds, which look and act like albatross. (San Francisco Maritime National Park Library.)

The USS *Pampanito* was launched in October 1943 at the Portsmouth Naval Shipyard in New Hampshire. The submarine sailed on her first patrol on March 15—a year to the day after her keel was laid. It made six patrols during World War II and is credited with sinking six Japanese ships and damaging four others. The officers and crew of the USS *Pampanito* posed for this photograph in San Francisco shortly after the end of the war in September 1945. (San Francisco Maritime National Park Library.)

The first woolen mill in California was built near the beach at Black Point Cove, known today as Aquatic Park. Pictured here around 1862, the San Francisco Woolen Mill manufactured uniforms for several armies in Europe, as well as flannels and blankets for the Union army during the Civil War. (San Francisco Maritime National Historical Park.)

The two cable car lines servicing Fisherman's Wharf are the Powell–Mason line, which began service in 1888, and the Powell–Hyde line, which started in 1891. This Powell–Hyde cable car is at the Beach Street turnaround, *c.* 1972. (Alessandro Baccari collection.)

In 1950, the Red and White Fleet ticket office opened at Fisherman's Wharf. Pictured here around 1972, adjacent to the east apron of Pier 45, are berths for the company's vessels. (Alessandro Baccari collection.)

In 1936, the Pan American China Clipper made one of its routine flights from San Francisco to Hong Kong. In the background is the skyline of the City by the Bay. Pier 39, pictured when ships of the General Steamship line berthed there, is below the plane. (Clyde Sunderland Foundation.)

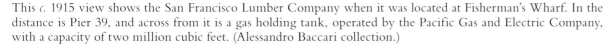

This *c.* 1915 view shows the San Francisco Lumber Company when it was located at Fisherman's Wharf. In the distance is Pier 39, and across from it is a gas holding tank, operated by the Pacific Gas and Electric Company, with a capacity of two million cubic feet. (Alessandro Baccari collection.)

In September 1982, the Fisherman's Wharf Merchant's Association honored Mrs. Hans (Friedel) Klussman for her efforts in saving the cable cars. Chairman of the luncheon was Christopher Martin, vice president of the association and administrator of The Cannery, owned by his family. (Fisherman's Wharf Historical Society.)

For many years, riders would help the Municipal Railway operators turn the cable cars around for the trip downtown from Fisherman's Wharf. In this August 1974 photograph is the turntable at Bay and Taylor Streets.

OPPOSITE: The famous Alioto brothers, who contributed greatly to the history of Fisherman's Wharf, are pictured here *c.* 1924, from left to right, (first row) Ignazio, Giuseppe, and Francesco; (second row) Nunzio, Salvatore, and Giovanni. (Paul Capurro collection.)

LEGENDS, HEROES, AND CELEBRITIES

Fisherman's Wharf's past is full of variety and color and singularly rich in human interest. No other part of San Francisco has a history more packed with incident, with contrasting epochs and swift, dramatic changes. Fisherman's Wharf is the by-product of the dreams and cultures of immigrants from many lands, but predominantly of Italian immigrants. There are many stories of those who contributed to the history of Fisherman's Wharf; individuals who have been called legends, heroes, and celebrities.

PIETRO PERAZZI, LEO TARANTINO, AND GRAGLINO ROSARIO: Old-timers still tell stories about Pietro Perazzi, Leo Tarantino, and Graglino Rosario. Partners and members of the fishing colony for over 30 years, they began working together in 1884 as the last of the felucca fishermen. It was said that two things were certain of these three patriarchs of Fisherman's Wharf—they would never give up arm power or sail for motor power, nor would they ever teach their tongues the English language. Their lives were circumscribed by North Beach and its inhabitants, who were predominantly Italian, and English was not necessary. Endurance and strength brought them fame. Imagine rowing and sailing to bring back sturgeon from the Sacramento River or journeying out on the Pacific Ocean to Half Moon Bay for salmon.

GIUSEPPE CAMILLONE: The "King Fisher of California," described by his fellow fishermen as "a man with the head of a leader and the neck of a blacksmith," came up with the idea in 1890 to replace feluccas with steam tugs. Today stories are still told of his generosity in aiding the families of fishermen who were in need of help to survive.

ACHILLE PALADINI: Paladini started as a felucca fisherman in the San Francisco fresh fish business in 1860, but later pioneered in the use of powerboats over sailboats. Before 1900, he was involved in the production, building, and outfitting of several trawlers for operation along the Pacific coast. In 1915, he was the first to can tuna in California, the first to smoke fish commercially, and the first to operate a cold storage plant. During the course of his illustrious career, he became a very controversial personality because of his monopolistic tendencies, though he was also known for his strong loyalties. After his death in 1921, his sons Alex, Attilio, and Hugo controlled much of the wholesale fish business for more than 35 years.

ANTONIO FARINA: In 1913, Farina was brought in by the independent crab fishermen to help them organize and establish a Crab Fishermen's Protection Association. At the time, they were battling for survival against the Fish Trust, which was made up of the five biggest fish companies on the Pacific coast and was able to fix prices. The Fish Trust enabled A. Paladini and Sons, the Western Fish Company, the International Fish Company, the Independent Fish Company, and Borzone Fish Company to control the commission rates and to carry out price fixing. With Farina's help, the Crab Fishermen's Protection Association rented a building on port property for the crab fishermen to unload their boats. For 21 years, with great success, Farina negotiated the purchase price for crabs with the fish brokers. He introduced many innovative programs for the benefit of the fishermen. He purchased gasoline in wholesale lots so fishermen could buy fuel at a lower price. He set up an insurance program for the fishermen. To care for the health needs of the fishermen and their families, he arranged for the Telegraph Hill Neighborhood Health Care Center to provide services. And since crab fishing was seasonal, he worked out an agreement with the Alaska Fish Packers Association to hire the independent crab fishermen during the off-season. He also set up Americanization classes to help the Italian fishermen become American citizens and brokered solutions—through business acumen and also by writing an insightful article for the weekly Italian language newspaper, *La Voce del Popolo*—to the sometimes-deadly conflicts that had for years soured relations between the crab fishermen and fish brokers.

LORENZO MANISCALCO: Acknowledged by all as the "King of the Crab Fishermen" for nearly 50 years, Maniscalco consistently brought to the wharf the biggest catch in the fleet. This stocky, barrel-chested man with a granitic, weather-hewn face was daring and brave, and his skills for crab fishing had no equal. He would pilot his *San Cristoforo* fishing boat out into the Pacific in weather that kept most boats moored to the dock. He would set his crab pots in areas of deep water next to rocky cliffs where the waves broke heavy and other fishermen dared not venture. Some say he could bring in as much as any two men on the wharf. What made his accomplishments so remarkable was that he always fished alone. In 1924, the Crab Fishermen's Protection Association honored him with a dinner and presented him with a gold medal on which was inscribed: "To Lorenzo Maniscalco, the champion, the Best Fisherman of them all." He continued fishing well into his 70s and died in 1973 at the age of 93.

HEROES OF THE WRECK OF THE SS *CITY OF RIO DE JANEIRO*: San Francisco experienced its worst maritime tragedy in the early hours on Friday, February 22, 1901, with the wreck of the SS *City of Rio de Janeiro*, a Pacific Mail Steamship Company liner, at the entrance to the Golden Gate. On that foggy morning, a group of fishing boats, including the *Newcomer* and *Andrea Doria*, headed towards the Gate. Among the skippers were Andrea Adami, Fred Castorini, Alberto Guino, Adamo Andrea, Matteo Mirabelli, and Spono Domini.

Cries of help could be heard through the fog, as Costa and De Jenaro spied floating debris and bobbing heads. In the distance, they saw a great black mass going down—the *Rio*. Fishermen from all the fishing boats aided in the rescue of the survivors. What clothes they had to share, they offered to those rescued to help them keep warm. The new Meigg's Wharf near Fisherman's Wharf had been turned into a rescue station. Many were the trips the fishing boats made from the scene of the wreck to Meiggs Wharf. The *Newcomer* brought 18 to safety on its first trip back to port; Andrea Adami saved 29 individuals in all, and the other boats accomplished similar heroic deeds. The *San Francisco Examiner* wrote, "The Italian fishermen were the first to the rescue and to the heroic and prompt action of these hardy toilers of the sea, many of the passengers and crew owe their lives." Of the 211 passengers and crew, 80 were saved.

JOHN NAPOLI: One day in August 1950, while returning to Fisherman's Wharf with 500 pounds of Pacific salmon on his 34-foot boat, the *Flora*, Napoli experienced the unforgettable. Through the fog, he thought he saw a large turtle in the water; it turned out to be a man bleeding and nearly unconscious. He brought him aboard. Minutes passed and as the fog began to lift, there, before his eyes, was a mass of bobbing heads. The SS *Mary Luckenback* and the navy hospital ship, *Benevolence*, which was on a trial run, had collided. The navy ship sunk. Approximately 526 men and women were aboard the hospital ship before it went down. Of the 498 men and women rescued, Napoli, by himself, saved 54, but at a dear cost—doctors later told him the exertion meant he could no longer do the physical work of a fisherman. He sold the *Flora* to pay his medical bills and died in 1969. The boat is still at the wharf as a reminder of Napoli's selflessness.

GIUSEPPE ALIOTO: "Alioto" is synonymous with Fisherman's Wharf, but no name stands out bolder than that of Giuseppe Alioto, who became a legendary figure in the fishing industry. Like so many, he got his start with the Paladini Fish Company, but began his own fish brokerage firm in 1908 at 539 Washington Street. From humble beginnings, Alioto's San Francisco International Fish Company became one of the leading fish companies in the nation by 1930, shipping fish throughout the U.S. in refrigerated railroad cars. Alioto also conceived of the Fish Trust and organized the Northern California Fisheries, an association of five major fish companies united to work together to eliminate large overhead costs brought about by the duplication of efforts in trawling, shipment, and the merchandising of products.

Alioto had six brothers and two sisters. Except for one married sister, all immigrated to America, and each of his brothers played a role in the fishing industry at the wharf. Ignazio, after working for F. E. Booth and Company, became president of the Consolidated Fish Company; John became a prominent lawyer and served as legal counsel for the Northern California Fisheries; Salvatore was manager of the Consolidated Fish Company; Frank, in partnership with his brother-in-law Tom Lazio, was president of the F. Alioto Fish Company; and Nunzio established Alioto's Restaurant, one of Fisherman's Wharf's finest. Mario, who died in his early 20s, worked for his brother Giuseppe at the San Francisco International Fish Company. Today Giuseppe Alioto is best remembered as the father of Joseph Lawrence Alioto, the 36th mayor of San Francisco.

RINA BOCCI: On January 30, 1942, a sweeping and far-reaching order went out that all aliens be removed from the waterfront district. The majority of people working at the wharf were Italian immigrants who were required to register as enemy aliens and carry photograph identity cards. They had to be 14 blocks away from Fisherman's Wharf. Large numbers lost their employment because of these restrictions; 1,400 out of 2,000 employed in the fishing industry at Fisherman's Wharf were affected by the order. Meanwhile, rumors flew that Italians would be evacuated as had Japanese, and daily warnings were issued that San Francisco, at any moment, might be bombed like Pearl Harbor.

It was a very frightening time, but through it all, there was Rina Bocci, director of the Italian Welfare Agency, who was there to help the Italian fishermen. She aided them in finding work, lodging, and getting medical and financial assistance. She even assisted in securing photograph identity cards for those who required them. For those hampered by language, she helped them in their dealings with the courts, the police, hospitals, and schools. During a very difficult and fearful time, Mrs. Bocci, for the Italian fishermen, was "an angel sent by God."

ROSA BATTAGLIA TARANTINO: According to legend, some fishermen lost in a storm were guided to safety by a light shining mysteriously from a grotto near Porticello. They found a framed fragment of marble of unknown origin bearing the Madonna's image, and the villagers carried it into town. Twice thereafter it vanished

and reappeared in the cave.

In 1935, Mrs. Tarantino organized the Maria del Lume Society, with the parishioners of Saints Peter and Paul Church, to commemorate this event and to bring faith to the fishermen and others facing hard times in the Great Depression. As the wife of a fisherman, she knew the perils of the sea and of the struggles to make a living from fishing. It was her belief that the spirit of tradition was needed to unite the fishing community at Fisherman's Wharf during the hard times and for holding dear the memory of those who had lost their lives to the sea. For the fishermen and their families, the event gave them reason to come together and celebrate, to share laughter and tears, and to pray that each year the fish would be plentiful.

Rosa Tarantino was a much-admired woman. She died on December 26, 1987, at the age of 95. The Blessing of the Fishing Fleet ceremony, which takes place each year, is her legacy to Fisherman's Wharf. During the first weekend in October, families of the fishermen gather on Saturday to attend a religious service at the Fishermen's and Seamen's Memorial Chapel, located adjacent to Pier 45 at Fisherman's Wharf. This is followed by a memorial service at sea. Family members board a Red and White Fleet harbor tour vessel for a journey that takes them just outside the Golden Gate. Participating in the journey are members of the fishing fleet. Prayers are said and floral wreaths are cast into the water from all the boats. The next day, there

is a Solemn High Mass held at Saints Peter and Paul Church followed by a procession, which bears a painting of the Madonna mounted on a flower-covered float with children aboard. Led by members of the Society of Maria SS del Lume, hundreds march the eight blocks from the church to Fisherman's Wharf. The pastor of the church then sprinkles holy water on the fishing boats and prays for abundance and protection.

JOE DIMAGGIO: Joe DiMaggio was born in Martinez, California, on November 29, 1914. He was the eighth of the nine children born to Maria and Giuseppe DiMaggio, who immigrated from Isola Delle Femmina, an islet off the coast of Sicily where the DiMaggios had been fishermen for generations. A year later in 1915, the family moved to San Francisco and lived in a flat on Taylor Street near Fisherman's Wharf where the elder DiMaggio docked his boat. Of the five boys in the family, two became fishermen and three—Vince, Joe, and Domenic—went on to become the greatest baseball-playing family in the history of the game. But only Joe became a baseball immortal—one of the greatest players to ever play the game.

While he was playing for the Sunset Produce team in one of the industrial leagues, professional scouts began to notice Joe's sensational batting power. Fred Hoffman, manager of the San Francisco Mission Reds, was the first to offer him a contract. This was followed by a contract from Spike Hennessey, a scout for the San Francisco

Seals. He was signed to a contract for $250 per month. During his first full season with the Seals at age 18, he broke all league records, hitting the ball safely in 61 consecutive games. In 1936, Joe signed to play for the New York Yankees. The first to welcome him to the big leagues was the team captain, Lou Gehrig. That year he hit 29 home runs, 15 triples, played in the all-star game, and became a member of a world championship team.

Joe's baseball greatness made him a national celebrity. On November 19, 1939, some 30,000 people crowded in front of Saints Peter and Paul Roman Catholic Church in San Francisco for his wedding to actress Dorothy Arnold. Out of the marriage came a son, whom Joe idolized. Five years later, while Joe Sr. was in the army during World War II, the marriage ended in divorce. Ten years later came the much publicized romance and marriage to film actress Marilyn Monroe. Unfortunately, it also ended in divorce.

Joe lived his life as he played baseball, with grace, dignity, and pride. In the twilight of his life, he found great pleasure in playing golf with old friends and was generous with his time with young athletes. His only major regret in life was that he could not help his son with his drug problem, which in the end claimed his son's life. Joe died on March 8, 1999, at the age of 85. He was an immigrant's son from Fisherman's Wharf who made it big as "the Yankee Clipper."

JOSEPH LAWRENCE ALIOTO: The son of Giuseppe, founder of the International Fish Company, Joe was born in San Francisco on February 12, 1916. He grew up along Fisherman's Wharf, helping with the chores at his father's fish company. While he enjoyed sports, especially basketball, young Joe was a brilliant student. He attended Saints Peter and Paul Grammar School, Sacred Heart High School, and St. Mary's College. In 1937, Joe graduated from St. Mary's with the highest academic honors and received a scholarship to attend the law school of Catholic University in Washington, D.C. Upon graduation from law school, he was invited to work for the antitrust division of the United States Department of Justice, which he accepted. During World War II, he was asked by the government to work for the Board of Economic Welfare where he helped evaluate the economic importance of bombing targets. In 1946, he returned to San Francisco and established what was to become one of the biggest antitrust firms in the nation. Among his first clients were Hollywood producers Walt Disney and Walter Wanger, for whom he won multimillion-dollar judgments that helped free up the nation's film distribution system. From 1964 to 1966, Alioto won more than $61 million in damages for his clients. He had become one of America's most celebrated attorneys.

It was by accident that Alioto became mayor in 1968. At the time, he was supporting state senator Eugene McAteer, one of two challengers trying to unseat mayor John Shelley. The other candidate was supervisor Harold Dobbs. McAteer tragically died of a heart attack while playing handball at the Olympic Club. Fearing that Mayor Shelley, a Democrat, would lose to Dobbs, a Republican, a number of leading Democrats urged Alioto to run. Shelly later withdrew due to poor health, and supervisor Jack Morrison entered at the request of Congressman Phil Burton, with the support of his powerful political machine. It became a three-way race, with Alioto winning in the end. Victory came, according to press at the time, because he overpowered his opponents with innovative ideas, a warm personality, dynamic energy, and oratorical and debating skills. Victory also brought him national attention as a bright new star in the Democratic Party.

After a flirtation with national politics, Joe returned to his San Francisco roots, where he left an impressive record as a reform mayor who actively mediated labor disputes, secured civil rights for minorities, lowered taxes, and brought economic vitality to the city. He took pride in the fact that he provided jobs for blue-collar workers and made San Francisco a workplace for hundreds of thousands of white-collar suburban commuters. As California senator Dianne Feinstein, herself a former mayor, said, "He truly made San Francisco into a big city." After a long battle with prostate cancer, Joe Alioto died on January 30, 1998, two weeks short of his 82nd birthday.

Joseph Balestrieri (left), a major fish broker at Fisherman's Wharf, is pictured here around 1938. One of his specialties was handling sardines. Here he is pictured with three outstanding sardine fishermen—Giuseppe Cresci, Giovanni Bellanti, and Machi. Until 1947, sardines were plentiful and a major source of revenue. (Fisherman's Wharf Historical Society.)

Joseph Lawrence Alioto, San Francisco's 36th mayor and one of America's most celebrated attorneys, grew up along Fisherman's Wharf helping with the chores at his father's fish company. With a charismatic style, he left his imprint on San Francisco and brought much pride to the community of Fisherman's Wharf. He is pictured here around 1970. (Tom Vano collection.)

Here is a view of San Francisco Bay, *c.* 1933, from lower Telegraph Hill. Pictured in the distance, from left to right, are Piers 37 and 39, PG&E's gas holding tank, and Pier 35. (Egizio Cuneo collection.)

Sardine fishermen from the A. Paladini Fish Company work the nets, *c.* 1938. (Egizio Cuneo collection.)

On April 28, 1913, the Marine Commercial Company hosted their second annual dinner for leaders of San Francisco's fishing industry. The event was held at the Rose Café. Among those in attendance were Giuseppe Alioto, president of the San Francisco International Fish Company; Attilio Paladini, son of Achille Paladini, founder of the A. Paladini Fish Company; and Frank S. Fusco of the Crab Fishermen's Protection Association. (Paul Capurro collection.)

The grand wedding of Ignazio Alioto and Frances Lazio on November 21, 1914, took place at Saints Peter and Paul Church. The reception was held at the Fior d'Italia Restaurant when it was located on Broadway Street in San Francisco. It is interesting to note that two of Ignazio's brothers married two of Frances's sisters, and her brother married one of Ignazio's sisters. (Paul Capurro collection.)

A get-together banquet of the trawling fishing captains, whose boats were berthed at Fisherman's Wharf, was held at Gianduja Restaurant on February 21, 1921. Each participant was a member of the Trawling Association. (Paul Capurro collection.)

The wedding of Joseph Paul DiMaggio to Dorothy Arnold at Saints Peter and Paul Church on November 19, 1939, had 30,000 people crowded inside and outside of the church. (Alessandro Baccari collection.)

Joe DiMaggio, an immigrant's son from Fisherman's Wharf, made it big as the "Yankee Clipper." Pictured here *c.* 1948, he lived his life as he played baseball—with grace, dignity, and pride. (North Beach Museum.)

This wedding photograph of Lorenzo Maniscalco and Maria Scafani was taken in 1905. He was the most legendary crab fisherman to hail from Fisherman's Wharf. (Dr. Joseph Maniscalco.)

The Blessing of the Fishing Fleet ceremony, which has taken place each year since 1936, is the legacy of a remarkable woman, Rosa Battaglia Tarantino (right). Her strongest supporter and helper was Rosa Alioto Castelloni (left). With this event, they made it possible for the fishermen and their families to come together and celebrate. Standing between Castelloni and Tarantino in this *c.* 1943 photograph is Rev. Fr. Thomas DeMattei, S.D.B., pastor of Saints Peter and Paul Church during World War II. (Alessandro Baccari collection.)

The independent crab fishermen of Fisherman's Wharf brought in Antonio Farina, a journalist, to help them establish a Crab Fishermen's Protection Association in 1913. They were battling for survival against the Fish Trust, made up of the five biggest fish companies. For 21 years, with great success, Farina (pictured here *c.* 1919) negotiated the purchase price for crabs with the fish brokers. (Ida Farina collection.)

Antonio Farina, general manager of the Crab Fishermen's Protection Association, would on numerous occasions take as his guests, members of the State Port Harbor Commission and their families, to the 1915 Panama Exposition and World's Fair. He would take them by fishing boat from Fisherman's Wharf to the fair, and during the trip, he would serve them cracked crab. (Ida Farina collection.)

Rev. Fr. Joseph Costanzo, S.D.B., served as pastor at Saints Peter and Paul Church twice—from 1944 to 1955 and from 1961 to 1969. During those 19 years as pastor, Father Costanzo was very supportive of the Blessing of the Fishing Fleet ceremony and took an active part in the celebration each year. Here he is shown blessing the fishing boats in 1962. (Charles Farruggia collection.)

For the fishermen of Fisherman's Wharf and their families, Saints Peter and Paul Church, pictured here in 1951, played an important role in their lives. It was there that their children were baptized, received First Communion, were confirmed, married, and buried. (Alessandro Baccari collection.)

Fishermen are at work around 1935 aboard a trawler fish boat owned by the Northern California Fisheries, a Fish Trust company established by Giuseppe Alioto with the support and participation of A. Paladini, Incorporated, Western California Fish Company, and F. E. Booth and Company. The headquarters for the Northern California Fisheries was located at the foot of Hyde Street at Fisherman's Wharf. (Egisto Cuneo collection.)

This 1915 photograph shows Fisherman's Wharf and a row of power crab boats. (Antone G. Cincotta Jr. collection.)

Live surplus crabs were often stored by the crab fishermen in wood crates and kept in the water of the Fisherman's Wharf lagoon next to one's boat. Pictured in this *c.* 1936 photograph is a fisherman removing crabs from a crate and sacking them for a buyer. (Egisto Cuneo collection.)

This *c.* 1915 view along the waterfront adjacent to Fisherman's Wharf shows a bustling northern waterfront industrial area with lumberyards, railroad tracks, and piers where lumber, livestock, wine, grain, and dairy products were unloaded. (Society of California Pioneers.)

The old Cuneo flats, located at Bay Street and Leavenworth Street, predominately housed newly arrived immigrant families from Sicily.

In January 1942, the U.S. government issued an order that all aliens be removed from the waterfront district. Fourteen hundred fishermen from Fisherman's Wharf were affected by the order. Motivated by determination and a deep religious faith, the Blessing of the Fishing Fleet ceremony took place nonetheless. (Frank Cresci collection.)

The name "Paladini" stands out in the history of the California fishing industry. For 100 years, the A. Paladini Fish Company controlled a good portion of the wholesale fish business, and its fishermen were always among the very best of those who fished along the coast of California. This image was taken around 1932. (North Beach Museum collection.)

A rare photograph of Fisherman's Wharf, *c.* 1919, taken from Russian Hill, shows the California Packers Cooperative in the foreground. The long building in the background (left) is the fish packing building that housed four major wholesale fish companies. Next to the cannery plant is the Standard Oil Company yards with petroleum tanks. Note the many lagoons for berthing fishing boats and the number of buildings on the piers to house the many boatbuilding shops. A standout is the long, wide wooden pier (upper left), which was used for unloading lumber, much of which came from the lumber mill in Mill Valley. The two buildings on the pier near the open water of the bay (right) are the U.S. Coast Guard building and the F. E. Booth Fish Company. (Fisherman's Wharf Historical Society.)

OPPOSITE: In 1900, Angelo Cannizzaro and his wife, Antonina, arrived from Porticello, Sicily, with five children to start a new life fishing at Fisherman's Wharf. Three more children were born in San Francisco. One of their children, Joseph Paul "Dolly" Cannizzaro, became a prominent leader in the community of Fisherman's Wharf. This photograph was taken around 1930. (Domenic J. Cannizzaro collection.)

PEOPLE AND BOATS GIVE THE WHARF ITS NAME

Fisherman's Wharf is an exciting place to visit because it is still very much a working fishing port. Thousands of tons of fish and the wharf's famous Dungeness crabs are still unloaded here each year. Gone, however, are the boat builders and the old "ways" used for repairing boats, the machine shops, and all but one of the ship chandleries. All have been replaced by retail stores and restaurants. Fear of retail expansion haunts the minds of preservationists who wish to keep the authenticity of Fisherman's Wharf. Worthy are those who aim to excel in tribute to the memory of those who came before, for their actions acknowledge their obligation of leaving for the next generation a place worthy of the one

they inherited. The following is a sampling of stories about individual commitment.

Carlo Joseph Cefalu is a master carpenter who spends his days repairing old Monterey fishing boats to pristine condition, as exemplified by his boat, the *Belle of Dixie*. This son of a fisherman laments that there are no more boat builders or ways for repairing boats at Fisherman's Wharf. "It's a shame they are forced out. Their outdoor work provided theatre for the visitors," stated Cefalu. "These boats will be around for the next generation to use and visually enjoy. Through them, the past lives on and that thought makes me happy," he commented.

The *Leonilda* belongs to fisherman Frank D'Amato, who doesn't fish daily anymore, but he was—or maybe still is—one of the wharf's great fishermen, especially for Dungeness crabs. D'Amato had hoped that his son would have been the skipper of the *Leonilda*, but that day never came for the ocean claimed him. So now, D'Amato spends his days at the wharf taking care of his beloved boat, occasionally going fishing and sharing his knowledge with the young, the next generation of fishermen. "Maybe one day, one of these young fishermen will be owner and skipper of the *Leonilda*, and when that time comes, the boat will be ready," stated D'Amato.

Robert Salvarezza and his wife, Alice, own Coast Marine and Industrial Supply, the last ship chandler at the wharf exclusively serving the fishing and boating industries. Since the age of eight, Robert Salvarezza has known most

of the fishermen at Fisherman's Wharf. They were introduced to him by his father, Mario, who took him when he went to sell netting and other supplies from the C. F. Hendry Company to the fishermen. While Mario sold to the boat owners, young Robert would make friends with the fishermen. As years passed, he and his father became partners in their own ship chandler operation, the Coast Marine Supply Company, later named Coast Marine and Industrial Supply. Even with the growth of the company, Robert's concern for the fishing industry never wandered. "The next generation of San Franciscans deserve to inherit a fishing industry at Fisherman's Wharf," expounded Salvarezza.

Stephanie Cincotta and her daughters Angela, Annette, and Mary Ann own and operate the Alioto-Lazio Wholesale Fish Company, which was established by her father, Tom Lazio, her uncle Frank Alioto, and Salvatore Tarantino. For over 100 years, the names of Lazio, Alioto, Tarantino, and Cincotta have been identified with the history of Fisherman's Wharf. Stephanie and her daughters strongly believe that the fishing industry is the heart which gives life to Fisherman's Wharf. This pride and attitude was strongly expanded during the trial preceding their court victory against the Port of San Francisco. These four remarkable women, fearful of the over-commercialization of Fisherman's Wharf and its threat to port property, have begun a campaign with T-shirts they made that read: "Keep the fish at Fisherman's Wharf."

One of the largest wholesale fish companies located at Fisherman's Wharf is California Shellfish, which was founded in 1948 by Robert Bugatto and Alfonso (Babe) LaRocca. The original name of the company was A. LaRocca Seafoods but it was changed due to the similarity to A. LaRocca and Sons. During the company's long history, space for expansion became necessary, so they discussed their needs with Miriam Wolfe, then port director, but at the time, she was actually contemplating the removal of the fishing industry from Jefferson Street. In addition, she refused to consider a long-term lease. So to meet their expanding needs, they opened a branch in Oakland and built a fish processing plant in Santa Rosa. The operation at Fisherman's Wharf remained what is has been— a receiving and distribution center. LaRocca's heirs have now sold their interest in the business to Gene Bugatto. Like his uncle and LaRocca, Gene believes in the future of Fisherman's Wharf and contemplates remaining there for many years to come. He acknowledges, however, that retail expansion is a threat to the fishing industry. He reviews the situation philosophically: "The port has given us long-term leases and has shown a willingness to support the fishing industry. We are encouraged by their actions. The next step is for the City, with port participation, to establish a master plan along with a traffic plan that will permit all businesses to exist in harmony. Uncontrolled retail expansion can destroy Fisherman's Wharf," stated Bugatto.

A. LaRocca and Sons wholesale fish company has been in operation since 1902. Founder Accursio "Leo" LaRocca was born in Sciacca, Sicily, in 1885 and migrated to the United States around the turn of the century with his sister and older brothers. At age 14, with the use of a wheelbarrow, he began selling crabs to restaurants on Columbus Avenue in North Beach and around downtown San Francisco. After a couple of successful years selling crabs, Accursio, now called Leo by his clients, had saved enough money to purchase a horse and buggy to replace the wheelbarrow. Soon the crab business became even more successful. After his two sons, Alfonso and Pasquale, were born, he proudly changed the name of the business to A. LaRocca and Sons. By now, trucks had replaced the horse and buggy, and Leo was soon called the "crab king." During the 1930s, the company expanded its operation to serve clients on the peninsula in San Mateo County and across the bay in Marin County, selling crab, live lobsters, fresh abalone, and Olympic oysters. Today the business is owned by his great grandchildren Michael, Nick, Paul, and Laura. Michael LaRocca is on the board of governors of the Fisherman's Wharf Merchants Association as a spokesman for the fishing industry. He also serves on the Port of San Francisco's Fisherman's Wharf Waterfront Advisory Group. According to LaRocca, "Challenges confronting the fishing industry will always exist. The industry must never lose sight of its goals or the importance it plays in the identity of Fisherman's Wharf . . . If the image, heritage, and economic vitality of Fisherman's Wharf is to be saved, a master plan is needed. Action must be taken now."

John Caito, president of Caito Fisheries, takes great pride in telling people that his family has been in the fish business at Fisherman's Wharf since 1885 when his grandfather, Baptista Caito, the patriarch of the family, opened a wholesale fish company under his name, after first making a living selling lemons and limes to tavern and restaurant owners. John Caito's other grandfather was Salvatore Tarantino who, with his brother, Peter, operated the fish brokerage firm of S. P. Tarantino and Sons, specializing in sardines, anchovies, and herring. The company was later renamed Western California Fish Company. John commented, "We are proud of our Caito heritage and that of our relatives who have contributed so much to the history of Fisherman's Wharf. Three sons and a daughter join me in the business and nine grandchildren await their turn. The fishing industry must be kept intact. Anything less there would not be a Fisherman's Wharf."

Of all the fleets operating on the bay, the oldest is the Red and White Fleet, founded by Tom Crowley Sr. Since 1892, the name Crowley has been synonymous with the history of San Francisco Bay. It all began when Crowley, at age 17, purchased a used Whitehall boat and entered the competitive boating business at the time. Within a year, he had three Whitehall boats and soon after, several gas-powered launches for moving goods and people from one county to another surrounding the bay. By 1906, the Crowley Launch and Tugboat Company was a leader in the field. Expansion continued with the purchase of sea vessels during World War I to carry goods between San Francisco, Australia, and South America. His influence continues to flourish in modern times. Crowley conceived the idea of harbor tours. During the 1930s, the main attractions were the construction of the Golden Gate and the San Francisco bay bridges and the 1939 World's Fair on Treasure Island. Since 1950, the Red and White Fleet has been operating from the wharf.

Crowley's grandson Tom Escher is the current owner of the Red and White Fleet, having previously worked as a sweeper and a mechanic's helper on the vessels. He plays an active role in the merchants association and serves on the Fisherman's Wharf Waterfront Advisory Group for the preservation and beautification of the wharf. "Fisherman's Wharf is a special place that brings pride to those who work there and joy to the visitors who come," he said. "Preservation must be a commitment by all."

Crab-cooking cauldrons, such as these pictured here around 1930, have been attracting people to Fisherman's Wharf for nearly 100 years. (Ron Ross collection.)

This is a *c.* 1910 portrait of the Antonio and Calagera (Linda) Rafello family. Daily hardships and hard work faced these two immigrants from Sciacca, Sicily, as they attempted to raise their family. Pictured, from left to right, are (first row) Maria, Augustino (Cresci), and Vincenzo; (second row) Francesca, Calagera, Antonio, and Emilio. Other children followed as well. (Vince Rafello Jr. collection.)

The Rafello Fish Market's stall No. 4 at Fisherman's Wharf is seen here in the mid-1920s. From left to right, are Vincenzo Rafello and his brother Stefano. (Vince Rafello Jr. collection.)

Sunday dinner at Grandma Rafello's home, *c.* 1932, with the children and grandchildren was a regular weekly event during the Depression years. Her home was located at 1333 Columbus Avenue near Fisherman's Wharf. The 1930s were hard times, but family spirit made them good times. No one was making money, but food was always on the table. (Vince Rafello Jr. collection.)

One of the pioneer families of Fisherman's Wharf is the Cresci family. Pictured in this *c.* 1931 photograph is fisherman Domenic Cresci with his wife, Carmela, and their children, from left to right, Nino, Peter, Mary, Rose, Frances, John, and Nick. (Domenic J. Cannizzaro collection.)

This wedding photograph of Frank Cannizzaro and Rose Cresci was taken around 1924. Each are from prominent fishing families from Fisherman's Wharf. (Domenic J. Cannizzaro collection.)

Luciano and Angelina Sabella celebrate their 43rd wedding anniversary, *c.* 1943, with 12 of their children. Luciano was one of the great felucca boat fishermen and his son, Antonino, established one of the landmark restaurants at Fisherman's Wharf—A. Sabella's Restaurant. (A. Sabella's Restaurant collection.)

One of the old fishing families of Fisherman's Wharf is the Cannizzaro family. Pictured in this *c.* 1900 photograph is Angelo Cannizzaro, his wife, Antonina Cresci Cannizzaro, and their eight children. Pictured, from left to right, are (first row) Frank, Angelo, Antonio, Antonina, and Joseph Paul "Dolly;" (second row) John, Peter, Rose, Mary, and Domenic. (Domenic J. Cannizzaro collection.)

The A. Sabella Fish Market was opened in 1920 by Antonino (Antone) Sabella. In this *c.* 1932 photograph, Antone (right) sets up the oysters and clams on trays with ice. Others in the photograph are his brothers, from left to right, Michael, John, Angelo, and Frank. (A. Sabella's Restaurant collection.)

Salvatore Guardino was the first fish peddler to secure a stall to operate a fish market on port property. Here, *c.* 1924, he is pictured selling crabs. (Alessandro Baccari collection.)

Here are members of the Crab Fishermen Protective Association. The gentleman wearing the white smock in this *c.* 1933 photograph is Salvatore Guardino, proprietor, along with his partner Giuseppe Licata, of the Excelsior Fish Market. Guardino served for many years on the board of directors of the association. (Alessandro Baccari collection.)

Here is the scene at Fisherman's Wharf in 1931. Note the cauldrons, with their tall chimneys, for cooking crabs. (San Francisco Maritime National Historical Park.)

The Excelsior Fish Market, established in 1915 by Salvatore Guardino and Giuseppe Licata, was one of the best places to buy fish and shellfish at Fisherman's Wharf. It closed in 1956. Today the location is a nautical souvenir store. Pictured in this 1930 photograph, from left to right, are Luigi Licata, Joe Licata, Peter Guardino, Vince Guardino, and Vince Licata. (Alessandro Baccari collection.)

During World War II, the Excelsior Fish Market was a busy place. Peter Guardino (in white) is preparing a live crab for cooking. Selling a fresh cooked crab to the lady is Vincent Guardino. (Alessandro Baccari collection.)

This is Fisherman's Wharf in 1920 when the fish markets along the west side of Taylor Street faced a wall of lumber across the street at the San Francisco Lumber Company. Pictured in this photograph are the two teenage Guardino brothers, Peter and Vincent (right), cooking crabs.

Displaced people were housed in "Camp 21" in Washington Square Park following the 1906 earthquake and fire. The barracks were up until the end of 1908.

The fish markets along Taylor Street are pictured here in 1938. (Fisherman's Wharf Historical Society.)

For 70 years, Tony Cresci sold crabs at Fisherman's Wharf. He began selling as a boy with his father, continued with his brothers, and was on his own in the end. Tony always wore the knitted fishing cap his mother made for him. He is pictured here inspecting fresh-caught crabs, *c.* 1980. (Alessandro Baccari collection.)

One of the most celebrated restaurateurs in the history of Fisherman's Wharf was Mike Geraldi, owner of Fishermen's Grotto No. 9, which he opened with his partner in 1936. Since the age of 10, Geraldi had been a fish peddler at Fisherman's Wharf. This photograph, taken in 1934, shows him selling crabs in front of the open space where his restaurant would be built.

Fishermen's Grotto No. 9 was among the first of the restaurants in San Francisco to work a reciprocal trade deal with a radio station for air time. Pictured here, *c.* 1947, is owner Mike Geraldi welcoming Carol Trotter, winner of the popular NBC program "Queen for A Day." A daily prize issued to each winner of the show was lunch at Fishermen's Grotto No. 9. (Fishermen's Grotto No. 9 collection.)

Every Saturday night, radio station KPO, the NBC outlet in San Francisco, would do a live broadcast from Fishermen's Grotto No. 9 Restaurant that featured Uncle Benny Walker's Amateur Hour program. In 1939, two individuals from Fisherman's Wharf won the grand prize—eight-year-old Peter San Filippo, nicknamed Joe E. Brown after the actor because of facial similarities, and Ignatio Balestrieri. San Filippo sang and Balestrieri played the accordion. Pictured in this *c.* 1939 photograph is young San Filippo playing the clappers, a handmade instrument. (San Filippo family collection.)

The wedding of Rose Passantino and Nunzio Alioto in 1915 was a major event; both came from influential Sicilian families. They had three children—Mario, Frank, and Antoinette. In 1925, they opened the N. Alioto Fish Company, along with a café, in the stall they leased from the state at Fisherman's Wharf. With the passing of time and hard work, that fish market and café blossomed into Alioto's Restaurant, one of San Francisco's finest fish restaurants. (Joey Alioto collection.)

In the operation of Alioto's Restaurant, most of the workers were family members. That was Rose Alioto's rule during her lifetime, and she encouraged her children to adopt that rule. This *c.* 1943 photograph from the Alioto family photograph album shows Rose (standing at left) with her children and relatives, welcoming home her son Frank, on leave from navy duty. (Joey Alioto collection.)

This is the northern section of the inner lagoon at Fisherman's Wharf before stalls Nos. 6 to 9 were built to house such establishments as the Alioto Fish Market, which later became Alioto's Restaurant, and Fishermen's Grotto No. 9. The building in the distance is the F. E. Booth Fish Company.

Fish are being unloaded around 1932 in the southern inner lagoon along the Taylor Street apron of the pier, where the fish markets and the Crab Fisherman's Protection Association building were located. (San Francisco Maritime National Historical Park Library, Charles Farruggia collection.)

Family and relatives gathered at the home of Vito and Rosa Machi to celebrate the Feast of St. Joseph on March 19, 1943, and to welcome home Peter Alioto, whose life had been spared when his ship was attacked and sank. Pictured, from left to right, are (first row) Stella Dal Toso, Gloria Machi, Frances Farruggia, Rosa Machi, and Frances Tarantino; (second row) Frank Machi, Vincenzina Alioto, John Billanti, Pietro Machi, and Vito Machi; (third row) Maria Crivello, Caterina Tarantino, Rose Alioto, Peter Selici, Rosa Tarantino, Rose Mary Clifton, Peter Alioto, Francesca Alioto, Frances Gustafson, Antoinette Alioto, and Rose Castelloni. (Charles Farruggia collection.)

Antonio "Hogan" Tedesco and Linda Franceschi opened the Sausalito Café in 1946. From the start, it became the place for commercial fishermen to eat. With the encouragement of the fishermen, they opened a small grocery store to provide provisions for the fishermen's needs when they went to sea. The Sausalito Café, pictured here c. 1948, later became Franceschi's Restaurant, known today as Capurro's Restaurant. (Paul Capurro collection.)

Frank Pompei and his wife, Marian, opened a small breakfast and lunch restaurant at Fisherman's Wharf in 1946, called Pompei's Grotto. This is a photograph of Pompei and what the establishment looked like in 1950. Enlarged and remodeled several times, the restaurant continues to be one of Fisherman's Wharf's most popular eating places. For many years, Frank Pompei served on the board of governors and as president of the Fisherman's Wharf Merchants Association. (Nancy Pompei Conyers collection.)

Here is the inner harbor of Fisherman's Wharf, *c.* 1940. In the background is Pier 45, Joe Tarantino's fish brokerage office and box house, Joe Balestrieri and Company's fish brokerage office, the Consolidated Fish Company, and Fishermen's Grotto No. 9 Restaurant. In the foreground are power fishing boats. (San Francisco Maritime National Historical Park Library.)

Shipping Dungeness crab to all corners of the U.S. was a big thing for visitors to Fisherman's Wharf in 1946, especially since crabs were sold for 50¢ apiece. One of the largest shippers at the time was Nunzio Alioto, owner of the N. Alioto Fish Company. (Frank Alioto collection.)

A panoramic view of the inner harbor of Fisherman's Wharf, such as this one from 1972, is what patrons are treated to when dining at Fishermen's Grotto No. 9. (Alessandro Baccari collection.)

The Vista Del Mar Restaurant, owned and operated by Ignazio Alioto and his family, was the upscale restaurant at Fisherman's Wharf when this photograph was taken in 1950. It was located on the second floor of what was once the Consolidated Fish Company. The manager of the restaurant was Pietro Pinoni, left. Pinoni was Alioto's son-in-law and, at the time, one of San Francisco's leading restaurateurs. (David Pinoni collection.)

The Buena Vista Café and Saloon, pictured here *c.* 1980 and located at the southwest corner of Hyde and Beach Streets, has been a San Francisco institution since 1895. The "B.V.," as it is often called, made history of sorts when it declared itself the first bar in America to serve Irish coffee. (Fisherman's Wharf Historical Society.)

The waters around San Francisco yield a delicious crustacean—Dungeness crab. They are sold fresh from bubbling cauldrons along Fisherman's Wharf. A woman is buying one such crustacean around 1975. (Fisherman's Wharf Historical Society.)

149

Here is the triangular parking lot along the Embarcadero, Taylor, and Jefferson Streets as it looked in November 1972. On the water side, one can see the Red and White Fleet bay cruise ships and ticket office, the Franciscan Restaurant, and Pier 4. The sailing ship *Balclutha* (formerly the *Star of Alaska* and now berthed at the Hyde Street Pier) and the Exposition Fish Grotto are on the right. (Fisherman's Wharf Historical Society.)

Three individuals highly respected by the community of Fisherman's Wharf, from left to right, are Rev. Fr. Louis Masoero, S.D.B., pastor of Saints Peter and Paul Church; Tomaso Castagnola, owner of Castagnola's Restaurant; and Joseph Paul "Dolly" Cannizzaro, owner of the Fisherman's Wharf parking lot. This gathering took place around 1970. (Domenic J. Cannizzaro collection.)

Pier J-10, located in the outer lagoon of the Fisherman's Wharf harbor, is pictured here around 1976. The wholesale fish companies, which worked off the pier when this photograph was taken, were Consolidated Fish Company, Alioto-Lazio Fish Company, California Shell Fish Company, and Standard Fish Company. (Alessandro Baccari collection.)

People are buying Dungeness crab at the N. Alioto crab stand on Taylor Street, c. 1935. (Frank Alioto collection.)

Scoma's Restaurant, pictured here around 1972 and located on Pier 47, is surrounded on all sides by fishing boats. It is one of the top money-making restaurants in America. (Alessandro Baccari collection.)

In this c. 1982 photograph, men are herring fishing in the San Francisco Bay. (Alessandro Baccari collection.)

High above the inner lagoon at Fisherman's Wharf, adjacent to Jefferson Street, stands Tarantino's Restaurant, pictured here *c.* 1972. It was opened in 1946 by Gene McAteer and Dan Sweeney, who referred to themselves as the "two Irishmen of Fisherman's Wharf." In 1958, McAteer became a state senator and William McDonnell came on board as a managing partner. The restaurant has become a Fisherman's Wharf fixture. It occupies space that once housed the Crab Fishermen's Protection Association, a legendary institution that played a vital role in the lives of the crab fishermen. (Alessandro Baccari collection.)

As World War II was ending in 1945, this cartoon of Fisherman's Wharf, which appeared in a San Francisco publication, was made by an artist named Vern. (Alessandro Baccari collection.)

The A. LaRocca and Sons Fish Company was established in 1902 by Accurrio (Leo) LaRocca and managed with the support of his sons Alphonse and Pat. The company became one of the major distributors of Dungeness crab at Fisherman's Wharf. This 1938 photograph shows Accurrio's grandchildren Leo LaRocca and Annette LaRocca Lippi, the children of Alphonse. (A. LaRocca and Sons Fish Company collection.)

Sales were up for the A. LaRocca and Sons Fish Company during the Depression years; trucking fish and shellfish to their customers in small refrigerated trucks throughout the San Francisco Bay Area was a major reason why. This photograph was taken *c.* 1938. (A. LaRocca and Sons Fish Company collection.)

In August 1947, the Fishermen and Ship Supply Company opened at 398 Jefferson Street at Fisherman's Wharf. Partners in the operation were Mario Salvarezza and Jack Jackson, two veterans in the chandlery marine trade. They began by buying up government marine surplus from World War II. Their sons, Bob Salvarezza and Dave Jackson, worked for their fathers until they were drafted into service for the Korean War. This photograph was taken on opening day. Pictured, from left to right, are Bob Salvarezza; his father, Mario; Hilda Jackson, bookkeeper (mother to Dave and wife to Jack); Dave Jackson; and Jack Jackson. The company is known today as Coast Marine and Industrial Supply, Incorporated and is owned by Bob Salvarezza and his wife, Alice. (Robert M. Salvarezza collection.)

With pride, Alphonse LaRocca, owner of the A. LaRocca and Sons Fish Company along with his brother Pat, shows off the new fishing boat, the *Crab King*, to his two children, Leo and Annette, in 1944. (A. La Rocca and Sons Fish Company collection.)

The Cincotta Bros. Marine Hardware and Fisheries Supply Company, pictured here around 1936, opened in the 1880s. Along with C. J. Hendry, it was one of the oldest chandlers in San Francisco. In 1969, it was bought by Bob Salvarezza and Coast Marine and Industrial Supply, Incorporated. (Antone Cincotta Jr. collection.)

This is the interior of the Cincotta Brothers Marine Hardware and Fisheries Supply Company, *c.* 1936, when it was located at 169 Jefferson Street at Fisherman's Wharf. (Antone Cincotta Jr. collection.)

In 1924, the Cincotta Brothers Marine Hardware and Fisheries Supply Company was located at 444 Bay Street. At the time, in addition to selling marine supplies to the fishermen, they also sold groceries and were a distributor for Dunlap tires as well. Pictured in the doorway are Antone Cincotta, left, and his brother John. (Antone Cincotta Jr. collection)

A fisherman mends his nets on a Sunday, *c.* 1949. Six days a week, they would fish. On the one day of "rest," this was always their chore. (Fisherman's Wharf Historical Society.)

Salvatore Tarantino, seen here in this c. 1908 photograph, was among the first major fish brokers at Fisherman's Wharf. Along with his brother Pietro, he specialized in buying and selling sardines, anchovies, and herring. His office was located in a single-room building on wharf J-3. Indoors or outdoors, he was never seen without his black derby. (Sal Tarantino collection.)

The Western California Fish Company, when the distribution center was located on the southeast corner of Powell and Francisco Streets and the company was run by the talented Anthony Caito, was a major leader in the fishing industry. This photograph was taken *c.* 1940. (John Caito collection.)

This vessel, one of many fishing boats owned and operated by the Western California Fish Company, was berthed at Pier 47 around 1931. (John Caito collection.)

One of the top fishing families during the 1930s was the Piazza brothers, pictured here *c.* 1936 unloading herring from their boat at Fisherman's Wharf. (Egisto Cuneo collection.)

Fisherman's Wharf had its share of rugged individuals who survived the Great Depression, such as these fishermen pictured here around 1936. (Egisto Cuneo collection.)

Antonino Alioto and one of his fishermen bring a boatload of herring into Fisherman's Wharf aboard his fishing boat, the *Golden Gate*, around 1938. (Sal Alioto collection.)

Longtime veteran fisherman Antonino Alioto repairs his gill net, *c.* 1938. (Sal Alioto collection.)

Monterey fishing boats are up on the ways for repairs and painting in this *c.* 1939 photograph. (Karl Kortum.)

Rows of crab pots line the decks of fishing vessels for the opening of the crab season in 1951. (Fisherman's Wharf Historical Society collection.)

Fishing outside the Golden Gate near Point Reyes, off the Marin County coast, *c.* 1938, are these fishermen from the Western California Fish Company. (Egisto Cuneo collection.)

This tug fishing boat, pictured *c.* 1902, was used by the Tarantino and Caito families to travel to Sausalito to escape the 1906 San Francisco earthquake and fire. The boat was owned by the Pietro Costa Fish Company, in which Baptista Caito had a financial interest. The Costa Fish Company was located on the Broadway Street Pier. (John Caito collection.)

Thomas Crowley (in bowler hat, center) has left his mark on the San Francisco waterfront. The companies he launched since 1892 have brought into use scow boats, tugboats, ferries, freighters, and bay cruise vessels. This *c.* 1905 photograph shows Crowley with his brother David at the Vallejo Street Pier discussing ticket sales of the river steamer *F. M. Smith*, which journeyed from San Francisco to Sacramento and back. (San Francisco Maritime National Historical Park Library collection.)

From the beginning, the Crowley Launch and Tugboat Company competed vigorously to become the largest operation of its kind on the West Coast. This 1905 photograph shows the use of a Crowley launching deck at the Vallejo Street Pier as sailors returned from an ocean voyage. (San Francisco Maritime National Historical Park Library collection.)

The Red and White Fleet ticket office at Pier 43, with its revolving, illuminated sign, has been a Fisherman's Wharf landmark since 1950. This photograph shows what the location looked like in November 1972. (Alessandro Baccari collection.)

Until 1974, there were still a few boat and machine shops servicing the fishing industry at Fisherman's Wharf, as illustrated by this photograph of the Boicelli and Mercury Shop taken in 1972. (Alessandro Baccari collection.)

San Francisco's Fisherman's Wharf is one of those rare locations where history, culture, and ethnic pride form a distinctive blend that gives it a strength and vitality all its own. This is a photograph of the wharf's outer lagoon adjacent to Scoma's Restaurant, *c.* 1972. (Alessandro Baccari collection.)

ACROSS AMERICA, PEOPLE ARE DISCOVERING SOMETHING WONDERFUL. *THEIR HERITAGE.*

Arcadia Publishing is the leading local history publisher in the United States. With more than 3,000 titles in print and hundreds of new titles released every year, Arcadia has extensive specialized experience chronicling the history of communities and celebrating America's hidden stories, bringing to life the people, places, and events from the past. To discover the history of other communities across the nation, please visit:

www.arcadiapublishing.com

Customized search tools allow you to find regional history books about the town where you grew up, the cities where your friends and family live, the town where your parents met, or even that retirement spot you've been dreaming about.

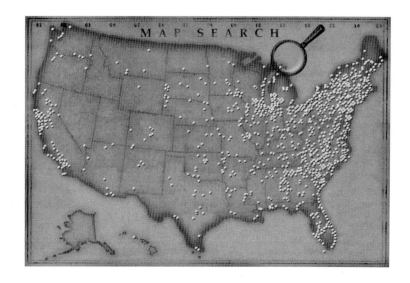